◆ IDENTITY AND ESSENCE

IDENTITY
AND ESSENCE

◆ ◆ ◆ ◆ ◆ ◆ ◆ ◆ ◆ ◆ ◆ ◆ ◆ ◆ ◆ ◆

Baruch A. Brody

PRINCETON UNIVERSITY PRESS
PRINCETON, NEW JERSEY

To
RICE UNIVERSITY
WHOSE
IDENTITY AND ESSENCE
MADE IT
THE RIGHT PLACE
AT
THE RIGHT TIME

♦ CONTENTS

◆ PREFACE

It is now close to fifteen years since I began working on the problems discussed in this book. At that time, these topics were not extensively discussed in the literature. It was before the publication of the ideas of Kaplan, Kripke, Lewis, Parfit, Perry, Plantinga, and so on. It was before the general recognition that there was a close connection between the philosophy of logic and classical metaphysics. Much has changed about the philosophical landscape in these fifteen years, and I hope that I have benefited in my work on these topics because of the new terrain laid out by these authors. It will be clear in the text how much I disagree with them. I hope it is equally clear how much I have learned from them.

The results of my earlier work have appeared in *The Journal of Philosophy*, *Nous*, *Philosophia*, *Philosophical Studies*, and *Philosophy of Science*. The interest in this work that had been shown by various members of the profession has encouraged me to complete this work, and I am thankful for this interest. As usual, my graduate students in various seminars at M.I.T. and at Rice have been very helpful; I only wish I could remember whom to thank for what. Because I cannot, I just want to thank them collectively for their many helpful suggestions. Finally, in dedicating this book to Rice, I am trying to express my feelings of immense gratitude for its being the type of university that it is. This book would never have been completed if I had not been in the supportive environment made possible by Rice's unique nature.

◆ **IDENTITY AND ESSENCE**

ONE ✦ THE THEORY OF IDENTITY FOR ENDURING OBJECTS

1.1 TOWARD A GENERAL THEORY OF IDENTITY

Problems concerning identity have been extensively discussed in the history of philosophy at least since Heraclitus worried about how anything could persist through change. In some cases, there has emerged something of a consensus. It is widely believed, for example, that spatiotemporal continuity is a necessary and sufficient condition for the identity of physical objects.[1] In other cases, there is an ongoing debate about the conditions for identity. Thus, philosophers are continuing the long-standing debate as to whether personal identity should be analyzed in terms of the identity of the relevant bodies or in terms of some sort of continuity of memory and character.[2] In still other cases, there are many philosophers who suspect that no account can be given of the identity of certain purported entities. Thus, some philosophers have claimed that no coherent account can be given for the identity of properties.[3]

These discussions about identity have substantial implications for many other issues. Many have argued, for example, that the theory of identity for physical objects rules out as incoherent certain radical proposals in contemporary physics about discontinuously moving particles or particles that move backward and then forward in time.[4] Such proposals, it is claimed, are incoherent just because they involve particle$_1$ at t_1 being identical with particle$_2$ at t_2 without p_1 being spatiotemporally continuous with p_2. Again, many have argued for or against the possibility of personal survival after bodily destruction on the basis of their theory of personal identity. Some have claimed that such survival is not possible because there can be no disembodied person p_2

at time t_2 identical with an embodied person p_1 at an earlier time t_1 just because personal identity is possible only when there is bodily identity.[5] Others have claimed, on the other hand, that such survival is possible because bodily identity is not required for personal identity.[6] Finally, some have argued that purported entities, like properties, should not be admitted into our ontology just because no coherent account can be given for the identity of properties.[7]

The first half of this book is a critique of this whole philosophical tradition. We shall argue that the tradition is based upon a fundamental erroneous assumption, and that once this assumption is shown to be in error, all philosophical problems in this area have to be rethought.

The assumption in question is that the truth-conditions of claims concerning identity vary as the type of entity in question varies. Thus, it is assumed that even if there is a satisfactory theory for the identity of physical objects, there can still be some doubt as to what is the best theory for the identity of persons, and it is questionable as to whether there can be any satisfactory theory for the identity of properties.

Let us analyze this assumption more carefully. There is no doubt that there is a difference between the truth-conditions of

(1) a is the same F as b

and

(2) a is the same G as b.

After all, for (1) to be true, a and b must both be F's but needn't be G's, while for (2) to be true, a and b must both be G's but needn't be F's. The assumption that I will be challenging is that there are sometimes further differences between the truth-conditions of such claims.

The version of the assumption that I will be concerned with (and that is widely held) is that when these additional differences are present, nothing can be both an F and a G. If, for example, there are further differences between the truth-conditions of

(1′) a is the same physical object as b

and

(2′) a is the same person as b,

then this is because nothing can be both a person and a physical object (although persons can have bodies that are physical objects). Again, if there are further differences between the truth-conditions of

(1″) a is the same property as b

and

(2″) a is the same set as b,

then this is because nothing can be both a set and a property.

There is a stronger version of this assumption according to which these additional differences are present even in some cases in which the same thing is both an F and a G. Thus, it is sometimes claimed that there is an additional difference between the truth-conditions of "a is the same train as b" and "a is the same collection of coaches and locomotives as b," even though the things in question (a and b) are both trains and collections of coaches and locomotives.[8] We shall not consider, however, the stronger version of this assumption, since it will certainly have little plausibility if the weaker version is undercut.

It is often said that disputes about identity-conditions are disputes about the nature of the objects in question, and that an understanding of the correct identity-conditions will lead to a better understanding of the nature of the objects in question. It is easy to understand why someone would say this, providing that, for many F's and G's, the additional identity-conditions for F's are different from the additional identity-conditions for G's. Then, one might well say that understanding these additional identity-conditions for F's (G's) sheds light upon the nature of F's (G's). If, however, we are successful in undercutting even the weaker version of this assumption about additional different identity-conditions, then the temptation to make these claims will be lessened. After all, if the conditions for the identity of *a* and *b* are the same no matter what type of objects *a* and *b* are, then it is unlikely that learning about the conditions for their identity will shed light upon the nature of the objects in question.

In any case, it is unclear as to why one should think that disputes about identity-conditions are disputes about the nature of the objects in question. Two dualists about persons might well, for example, disagree about identity-conditions for persons, one holding a bodily theory and one holding a psychological theory, and two proponents of the bodily theory of personal identity might disagree about the nature of persons, one being a materialist and the other being a dualist. Many more examples can be given. So there is no reason to suppose that disputes about identity-conditions are disputes about the nature of the objects in question. And if we succeed in undercutting the assumption, this will be perfectly clear.

How will we challenge this assumption? Our strategy is very simple: in the opening two chapters, we will present and prove the adequacy of a general theory of identity, one that involves no additional differences in the truth-conditions. In Chapter Three, we will then show how this general theory undercuts the traditional additional truth-conditions, and that this explains why traditional identity-theories were forced to a variety of unsatisfactory conclusions. Our conclusion will, therefore, be that there is no need to develop any special theories of identity in order to have a necessary and sufficient condition for the identity of any entities, and that the theories that have been developed are false.

1.2 THE IDENTITY OF INDISCERNIBLES AS A GENERAL THEORY

In second-order logic, the following axioms are usually presented as the basis for the theory of identity:

$$(x) \ (x = x) \tag{1}$$
$$(x) \ (y) \ (F) \ [(x = y) \supset (Fx \equiv Fy)] \tag{2}$$

These axioms are general axioms, that is, they hold for entities of all types. But they do not provide us with a full theory of the truth-conditions for identity-claims since they only provide us with necessary conditions for the truth of identity-claims.

The general theory of identity that I will be defending is based upon the theory that results when one adds to those two axioms the additional principle of the identity of indiscernibles, the principle that

$$(x) \ (y) \ [(F) \ (Fx \equiv Fy) \supset x = y] \tag{3}$$

This principle says that x and y are identical if they have all of their properties in common.

What then is our theory? Well, consider the claim that a is the same F as b. According to our theory, that claim is equivalent to the claim that a and b are F's and $a = b$ and is true if and only if a and b are F's and have all of their properties in common. Now consider the claim that a is the same G as b. According to our theory, that claim is equivalent to the claim that a and b are G's, and $a = b$ and is true if and only if a and b are G's and have all of their properties in common. In short, according to our theory, there are no additional differences in the truth-conditions of identity-claims because (1)–(3) provide us with a general theory of the truth-conditions of the identity part of identity-claims.

We can also put our theory as follows: we can distinguish two parts of claims like (1) and (2). One part is the assertion that a and b belong to a given type of objects. Naturally, the truth-conditions of this part of the claim vary as the type in question varies. The other part is the assertion that a and b are identical. What our theory claims is that the truth-conditions of this part of the claim are the same no matter what the type of the entities in question; a and b are identical just in case they have all of their properties in common. We can even turn that into a definition of identity:

$$x = y =_{\text{def.}} [(F) \ (Fx \equiv Fy)] \tag{4}$$

Before proving the adequacy of this account, we must make certain explanatory points about this definition: first, the domain of the quantifier "(F)" is the class of all properties. There are some who understand "property" in a restrictive fashion.[9] According to them, a property must be applicable to more than one object; if only one object can have the "property" in question, it isn't really a property. Now, I have no developed general theory of propertyhood on the basis of which I can argue that this restriction is inappropriate. All that I can say is that, when I talk about properties, I will be referring inter alia to entities that can only be applied to one object. In my terms, for example, "being the first person to walk on the moon" designates a property, even though the property in question can only be had by one object. (Roughly speaking, but only roughly, the justification for this is that a property is something that is had by an object, and that only one object can have the property in question does not, therefore, count against its being a property.) Second, this general definition does commit us to inferring, when Frank = the president, the truth of

(i)   John believes of the president that he is a good guy

from the truth of

(ii)   John believes of Frank that he is a good guy,

even though John, who is mistaken about who is president, believes that the president is a bad guy.

(ii) and (i) ascribe the same property to the same object, and (i) must be true if (ii) is. This becomes perfectly all right as soon as one distinguishes (i) from

(iii)   John believes that the president is a good guy,

which is false in our imagined tale because it does not ascribe the same property to the same object as does (i) and (ii). Assertions (i) and (ii) ascribe to Frank (the president) the property of being such that John believes of him that he is a good guy. Assertion (iii) ascribes to John the property of believing a certain proposition to be true (or to a certain proposition the property of being believed in by John, or to the pair the relevant relational property), and its truth does not follow from our definition and the truth of (i) and (ii).

Now for the proof of the satisfactoriness of our definition. The necessity part, which is really Leibniz's Law, has been widely accepted by philosophers. The only hesitations about it are due to worries about belief-properties and modal properties, and it is now generally recognized that these worries are ill-founded in light of the distinctions that we have just discussed [viz. the distinctions of the type exhibited by the distinction between (i) and (iii)]. What is much more controversial, and requires proof, is the sufficiency for identity of a having the same properties as b. But the proof of that is really trivial:

(i)   Suppose that a and b have all of their properties in common

(ii) a certainly has the property of-being-identical-with-a

(iii)   so, by supposition, does b

(iv)   then $b = a$.

There are two types of objections that might be raised to this proof. One of these objections, that this proof reveals the triviality and/or circularity of our definition, will be dealt with in Sections 1.3 and 1.4. The other objection, which we should consider now, is an objection to (ii).

How can one object to (ii)? At first glance, it seems to follow directly from the trivial logical truth that $a = a$. If $a = a$, it would certainly seem to follow that a has the property of-being-identical-with-a. Nevertheless, someone might want to object to (ii) even while granting that $a = a$. Such a person would be claiming that even though it is true that $a = a$, it does not follow that a has the property of-being-identical-with-a. Why not? It would seem that the only way to make that claim would be to argue that there is no property of-being-identical-with-a. But how could one argue for that claim? Two suggestions come to mind:

First, there is no property of-being-identical-with-a because properties are such that it must at least be possible that more than one object have them, and being-identical-with-a could not be possessed by more than one object; if this is the argument, then we can disregard it because we are using the notion of a property in a wider sense in which there can be properties which are such that they can only be possessed by one object.

Second, there is no property of-being-identical-with-a, just the more general property of self-identity; if this is the argument, then I believe we can nullify it by considering carefully the basis we have for believing in the existence of any given property. The existence of properties is postulated in the realist account of truth; sentences are true just because certain objects have certain properties. Now suppose that it is true that $a = a$ but false that $c = a$. What property is it which a has but which c lacks that makes the first claim true and the second false? It cannot be the general property of self-identity, since both a and c have that property. It must, I submit, be the property of-being-identical-with-a. So the second objection should also be rejected.

1.3 THE TRIVIALITY OBJECTION (I)

Many have objected that this definition of identity, and the principle of the identity of indiscernibles upon which it is based, is either trivial or circular. Their claim is naturally reinforced by the proof that we have just offered, since it certainly involves the very property that is being defined. Nevertheless, this objection, despite its popularity, is in error.

Let us begin with the question of triviality, looking first at the familiar argument put forward by Ayer[10] and O'Connor.[11] The argument begins as follows:

At this point, however, some indication must be given as to what is, or at any rate what is not, to be counted as a predicate. For if no restriction is placed upon the type of predicate to be admitted, our rule very easily becomes trivial. Thus if A is allowed to have the property of being identical with itself, it is clear that there will be at least one predicate which will not be included in any set of predicates applying to something other than A, namely the predicate of being identical with A.[12]

In one way, this claim is obviously correct. It is indeed trivial to prove, given a wide understanding of "property," that the identity of indiscernibles is true and that (4) provides a perfectly adequate set of necessary and sufficient conditions for the identity of any objects. In another way, however, this claim is in error. It strongly implies that this triviality is objectionable, but it fails to explain why it is objectionable.

One might think of this issue as follows: those who raise the triviality objection might think that the triviality is objectionable either because they suppose that the adequacy of any definition of identity should not be trivially provable, or because they suppose that any definition whose adequacy is trivially provable could not do the philosophical work that is needed. The former reason seems to be nothing more than a masochistic desire for hard work. The latter reason makes more sense, but of course no grounds are given for believing that such a definition would have uninteresting philosophical consequences. Moreover, the rest of this book will show, I hope, how unfounded is that belief. I shall be arguing implicitly throughout this book that the adoption of this definition whose adequacy is trivially provable leads to a rethinking of a considerable number of philosophical issues. If my arguments are correct, then this worry about triviality can be laid to rest.

The circularity objection is much more substantial. After all, consider definition (4) and suppose, as we do, that identity-properties are included in the scope of the quantifier. Wouldn't we then have defined identity in terms of itself, and wouldn't our definition then be circular?

I think not. After all, our definiendum ("identity") does not occur in our definiens ("that relation which holds between x and y just in case they have all of their properties in common"), and so our definition cannot be circular. To be sure, we have defined "identity" in terms of itself insofar as we have defined it in terms of a totality (the totality of properties) to which its referent belongs, but that makes the definition impredicative and not circular. We shall now show that there is nothing wrong with such an impredicative definition, either from the perspective of understanding the definition or from the perspective of subsequently coming to know that objects x and y are identical.[13]

Let us first consider the question of understanding our impredicative definition. In order for someone to understand it, they would have to know (although not necessarily be able to explain) (a) what a relation is, (b) what it is for a relation to hold between objects x and y, and (c) what it is for objects x and y to have all of their properties in common. Since, apparently, one can know all of this without knowing what relation the relation of identity is, someone could learn, on the basis of this definition, what relation "identity" stands for. Since this is so, an impredicative definition like ours, unlike a circular definition, is perfectly satisfactory from the perspective of coming to understand it.

Some might feel that knowing (c) requires knowing which relation identity is. After all, it might be said, in order to know what it is for objects x and y to have all of their properties in common, one would have to know all of the properties in question, and if identity-properties are among the properties in question, then one would have to know which relation identity is. I cannot agree with this line of reasoning. After all, there are many properties of objects that none of us know about, and yet that does not prevent us from understanding the general notion of objects sharing all of their properties in common. So why should we have to know what relation the relation of identity is in order to understand the general notion of objects x and y sharing all of their properties in common?

This point can also be put as follows: what enables us to understand the proposed definition of identity is our understanding of certain general terms such as "relation" and "sharing a property in common." Since our impredicative definition only employs these general terms, it can be understood by those who want to learn the meaning of "identity." This is why our definition does not suffer from the defects of circular definitions.

But is this definition satisfactory from the perspective of subsequently coming to know that objects a and b are identical? Wouldn't any attempt to come to know that a and b are identical encounter difficulties akin to those produced by circular definitions? After all, in order to know that a and b are identical, we will first have to know whether they have all of their properties in common. And since a has the property of-being-identical-with-a, we will, therefore, first have to know whether b also has that property; we will, therefore, first have to know whether b is identical with a. So in trying to learn whether a and b are identical, we will come about in a circle, and our definition, therefore, raises insurmountable problems for our knowledge of identity.

Even this plausible-sounding objection is in error. To be sure, to know that a and b are identical is to know that they have all of their properties in common. But this neither entails that we know the latter before the former, nor that we first have to check out every property that one has to see that the other has it as well. In particular, it does not entail that we must first check b to see whether, like a, it has the property of-being-identical-with-a.

But then how do we come to know that a and b are identical? One very common way seems to be the following: we look at some of their properties, see that they have them in common, and infer that they have all of their properties in common—that they are identical. What type of inference is that? Well, if the properties in question include one—other than identity properties—that two different objects cannot share, then the inference in question is a deductive inference. If no such property is included in the set of properties in question, but the set in question is such that it is unlikely that two different objects would share it, then we infer that a is identical with b as a way of simplifying our explanatory account of things. We simplify our explanatory account of things by identifying a and b, for then we do not have to explain how they come to share a set of properties which are such that it is unlikely that two different objects share it.

This last point, by the way, shows what is wrong with one of Professor Wiggins's arguments against the identity of indiscernibles as an effective sufficient condition for identity:

It is not effective (i) because, for any identity $a = b$, there will be many predicates whose application to one or another of a and b can only be settled by first settling whether $a = b$. . . .[14]

The argument seems to be the following: (a) using (3), we could only show that $a = b$ by establishing that they have all of their properties in common; (b) in order to do this, we would first have to check all of them; (c) we cannot check many of them without first knowing whether $a = b$. As is clear from our discussion above, step (b) is in error. Wiggins might, no doubt, reply that there are not in general enough properties whose common instantiation by a and b could be established, independently of establishing whether a and b are identical, to justify the inference that they are identical. But this strong claim, unlike the innocuous (c), needs justification, one that Wiggins does not provide and one that does not suggest itself. So, unless Wiggins presents some other arguments, his objection to (3) collapses.

1.4   THE TRIVIALITY OBJECTION (II)

In the last section, we defended the identity of indiscernibles on the assumption that the quantifier in its expression that ranges over properties ranges over all properties. And it is this version of the principle that we will employ in the rest of the book. Nevertheless, because it has some independent interest, I should like to consider the following question: would the identity of indiscernibles still be true if we excluded identity-properties from the domain of that quantifier? Now, it certainly would be true if the following two assumptions were true: (a) the domain contains properties that can only be had by one object at one time, and (b) each object would still have at least one such property. But would these assumptions be true?

Let us begin by considering concrete objects, objects that are spatiotemporally located. It would seem that, for each concrete object, there is one property (the property of being in a particular place—which place varies, of course, from object to object) that only it has at a given time. Or, to put this point another way, since two concrete objects cannot be in the same place at the same time, it would seem that (a) would be true and (b) would be true at least for concrete objects.

The trouble with this argument is that it presupposes that two concrete objects cannot be in the same place at the same time, and that supposition is false. Consider, for example, me and my body. At least as long as I am embodied, my body and I are in the same place at the same time, and yet we are not identical. Or consider a ball that is growing hot and rotating simultaneously, and consider the event of its growing hot and the event of its rotating.[15] They are in the same place at the same time, and yet they are not identical. In short, it seems that being in some particular place at some particular time is not a property that necessarily is had uniquely.

Locke, who was well aware of this problem, thought that it could be solved because he believed that all concrete objects are divisible into several classes which are such that no more than one member of a given class could be in a given place at a given time.[16] Then each concrete object would uniquely have the property of being the member of a given class in a given place at a given time. Whatever the merit of this general approach, Locke's own list of classes—God, physical objects, and finite spirits (people)—will not do because it does not cover all concrete objects. It leaves out, for example, events. Moreover, and this is the more serious problem, this approach cannot be solved merely by adding to the list a few more entries like events. As Davidson's example shows, two events can be in the same place at the same time.

Perhaps the following suggestion might be satisfactory: although possessing a given location at a given time is not necessarily a uniquely held property, no two objects that have all of their other nonidentity properties in common can be in the same place at the same time. I and my body can be in the same place at the same time and not be identical because there are many nonidentity properties that we do not share (for example, while I am thinking about identity, my body is not). The growing hot of the ball and the rotation of the ball can be in the same place at the same time because there are many nonidentity properties that they do not share in common (for example, the former is taking place at a rate of 50°F. per minute, while the latter is not). Can we not then say that the full set of properties of any concrete object, including its spatiotemporal locations but excluding its identity properties, are had by it uniquely? And can we not, therefore, say that condition (b) would be satisfied for every concrete object by the property of having that set of properties?

This suggestion may be correct; it certainly can handle the familiar counterexamples, and I cannot think of any new ones. Still, I am troubled for this reason. According to this suggestion, there could be two objects A and B in the same place and exactly alike (leaving aside identity-properties) except that A has a property P and B has not. Suppose that this was so. What could prevent B from acquiring that property? Suppose it did, would it then be identical with A? How could it be? Would it then have gone out of existence and only A remains? Why should its acquiring P require it to go out of existence? So, it looks as though, contrary to the proposal, there could be, leaving aside identity-properties, two objects in the same place at the same time with exactly the same properties. Perhaps another way of putting this same point is this: there is something intuitively acceptable about Locke's idea that two objects of the same type cannot be in the same place at the same time; but the claim that is advanced in this suggestion, which allows two objects of the same type to be in the same place at the same time but insists that they must differ in some accidental properties, lacks any intuitive backing. So, despite the absence of counterexamples, I am reluctant to depend upon it.

It remains an open question as to whether spatiotemporal properties, or perhaps some other type of properties, will make (b) true for all, or even some, concrete objects. What about abstract entities? Here we seem to be in better shape. Consider, for example, numbers. Any number is the unique object that is the sum of, or difference between, two other numbers. So any number has at least one property uniquely, the property of being the sum of (or difference between) the two other numbers in question. Similarly, each set has at least one property uniquely, the property of containing all and only certain objects; each statement has at least one property uniquely, the property of asserting of a given object that it has a given property; and so on.

It should be noted that we have not made use of lots of other uniquely held properties, like the property of being the first man to land on the moon, the property of being the only number that John is superstitious about, and so on. While there certainly are such properties, and while many of them certainly are instantiated, we have no guarantee that every object instantiates at least one of them. That is why we looked for classes of uniquely held properties, ones whose different members are uniquely had by the different members of some broad class of objects.

In short, even if we disregard identity-properties, the identity of indiscernibles is certainly true for many types of objects, and may well be true for all of them. In any case, there is no reason to disregard them, and then the identity of indiscernibles is provably true for all objects.

1.5 The Objection from the Paradoxes

It is sometimes claimed that adopting the identity of indiscernibles or our definition of identity—especially if one does so by quantifying, as we have, over all properties—leads one into paradox. Thus, Professor Geach argued as follows:

> But if we wish to talk this way, we shall soon fall into contradictions; such unrestricted language about "whatever is true of a," not made relative to the definite ideology of a theory T, will land us in such notorious paradoxes as Grelling's and Richard's. If, however, we restrict ourselves to the ideology of a theory T, then, as I said, an I-predicate need not express strict identity, but only indiscernibility within the ideology of T. [17]

I find this argument very strange. Consider, for example, Grelling's Paradox. We learn from it that the property of being a heterological property, if there is such a property, is itself neither heterological nor autological. But how are we forced, by our theory of identity, to assert that it is one or the other? Why cannot we say, as do many others, that there is no such property, or that there is but it is neither heterological nor autological? In short, why does talking of all of the properties of an object in any way lead us into paradox?

It might be thought that we are at least led into set-theoretical paradoxes. After all, we have a quantifier ranging over all properties. Doesn't that mean that we have a set of all properties, and doesn't that mean that we have a set that is "too large" and that gives rise to paradoxes? Once more, I do not see that this result follows. To begin with, does the use of a quantifier necessarily commit us to the existence of a set over which it ranges? Is that, after all, the only way to interpret the quantifier? More importantly, why can't the quantifier range over a proper class, and not a set? That is sufficient to avoid the paradoxes.

In short, then, our theory of identity is not ruled out by its leading to any paradoxes.

1.6 BLACK'S COUNTEREXAMPLE

We turn now to Professor Max Black's claim that there are possible counterexamples to the identity of indiscernibles and to our resulting definition of identity. Black describes his case as follows:

> Isn't it logically possible that the universe should have contained nothing but two exactly similar spheres? . . . every quality and relational characteristic of the one would also be a property of the other. Now if what I am describing is logically possible, it is not impossible for two things to have all their properties in common.[18]

At first sight, this argument seems unconvincing. After all, if there are two such objects, then each is such that there is an object with which it and only it is identical. So each must have a unique property, even if we cannot specify the property because (as Black reminds us) we have no way of specifying the object. Black would not, of course, be moved by this objection, since he argued that we cannot consider such identity-properties: "If you want to have an interesting principle to defend, you must interpret 'property' more narrowly-enough so, at any rate, for 'identity' and 'difference' not to count as properties."[19] But as this is nothing more than the triviality objection, we need not consider it any further.

There is, however, another point that should be noted here. Let us disregard, for a moment, identity-properties. Black claims that the possibility of his universe shows the falsity of the identity of indiscernibles. But has he actually described a possible counterexample? There is, to be sure, nothing wrong with his description insofar as it asserts that the universe in question contains a sphere a having certain properties, and a sphere b having the same properties. But is the description still coherent when Black adds that a is not identical with b, that there are two such spheres? Isn't Black just begging the question when he claims that it still is coherent?

Black, it should be noted, assesses the situation differently. He says: "I tried to support my contention that it was logically possible for two things to have all of their properties in common by giving an illustrative description. . . . It was for you to show that my description concealed some hidden contradiction. And you haven't done so."[20] I fail to see his point. The issue is not on whom the burden of proof lies. It is about whether Black's having provided a description accomplished anything, given that the question of the coherency of his description boils down to the question of the truth of the identity of indiscernibles. It seems that it should not.

This last point raises a general question about the use of possibilities as counterexamples to philosophical claims. Suppose that a philosopher claims that p is necessarily true (for instance, that indiscernible objects are necessarily identical), and suppose that another philosopher offers a possible case in which p is not true. Has the second philosopher accomplished anything? Isn't it open for the first philosopher to reply that the question is being begged when it is assumed that the case is a possible case? It would seem that this familiar technique, which Black employed here, is not as useful as many think it is. But we shall return to this general issue in Chapter Three.

1.7 IDENTITY THROUGH TIME

All of the objections that we have considered so far claim that our entire theory is mistaken. The final objection that we will consider maintains that our theory is correct but incomplete. It runs as follows: there are two different problems for a theory of identity, the problem of the truth-conditions of identity claims involving objects that exist at the same time (the problem of identity at the same time), and the problem of the truth-conditions of identity claims involving objects that exist at different times (the problem of identity through time). Even if our theory is a correct theory of identity at the same time, it is incomplete because it is not a correct theory of identity through time. After all, an object can change some of its properties over a period of time and still remain the same object numerically. Thus, my table which is red at t_1 can be black at t_2 and still be the same table. My table at t_1 is identical with my table at t_2, but they do not have all of their properties in common. So having all of their properties in common is not a necessary condition of identity through time, even if it is a necessary condition for identity at the same time. Similarly, there must be some new sufficient condition for identity through time that my table at t_1 and my table at t_2 satisfy. In short, the objection runs, the general theory of identity that we have presented is incomplete; it has to be supplemented by a theory of identity through time, and that theory may not be a general theory.

It seems to me that there are fundamental difficulties with both of the assertions of this final objection: with its claim that there are two different theories of identity, and with its claim that the theory of identity at the same time is inadequate as a theory of identity through time. Let us consider the former claim first.

Let a be some object that existed (exists, will exist) at t_1, and let b be some object that existed (exists, will exist) at t_2. Either a also existed (exists, will exist) at t_2 and b also existed (exists, will exist) at t_1, or not. In the latter case, a and b are clearly not identical. After all, how can the same object both exist and not exist at the same time? In the former case, a and b are objects existing at the same time, and any theory of identity at the same time is a theory of their identity. So we can see that there is just one theory of identity.

But what about the argument that was offered to show that there is a need for two different theories, that a satisfactory theory of identity at the same time is not a satisfactory theory of identity through time? That argument rested on a straightforward error. What is required by indiscernibility is that my table at t_1 and my table at t_2 have the same properties at t_1 and the same properties at t_2. It is not required that my table at t_2 have at t_2 the properties that my table at t_1 had at t_1. So it is irrelevant to indiscernibility that my table at t_1 was red at t_1 while my table at t_2 is black at t_2. To put this point another way, what our theory says is that a and b are identical just if, at any given time, they have the same properties at that time. And if my tables are the same table, they will satisfy that condition even though my table at t_1 was red at t_1 and my table at t_2 is black at t_2.

Let me add at this point one brief epistemological note. As we have just seen, there is nothing in our theory that requires that b at t_2 have at t_2 any of the properties that a at t_1 had at t_1 in order for b to be identical with a. Nevertheless, if b's properties at t_2 are radically different from a's properties at t_1, then this will usually be taken as evidence that b is not identical with a. That this is so does not, I submit, require any change in our theory of identity; we can explain it as due to our knowledge that things do not (at least usually) change radically over time. But we shall return to this point in Chapters Four and Five of the book.

Those who have raised the objection about identity through time would not, I believe, be moved by our reply. They would, I suspect, say something like this: when we talk about a existing both at t_1 and at t_2, we are already employing the notion of identity through time, which is what we are supposed to be explaining. Our reply, they would claim, really begs the question. They might also put their reply this way: let us introduce the notion of a stage as a momentary object. Stages are in many ways different from enduring objects; stages do not persist through time, and cannot therefore change. Still, the idea of an enduring object must be constructed out of the idea of a stage. We have to explain what it is for a set of stages to form an enduring object. That is the problem of identity through time which our theory fails to handle.

This counterreply can be met at a number of levels. One thing that one can say is that its claims are literally incorrect. To talk about an object as existing at more than one time, all that we have to say is that $(\exists t_1)(\exists t_2)$ (a is at t_1 and a is at t_2 and $t_1 < t_2$ or $t_1 > t_2$), and none of this requires the notion of identity. All that it does require is names for enduring objects. And given that we can directly name enduring objects, we don't have to introduce these names as the name of a set of stages. But to do justice to this counterreply, something deeper has to be pointed out.

In any metaphysical program, whether one views it as constructing some concept out of others or analyzing that concept into others, one always begins with certain machinery. What I have been arguing is that if we begin with second-order logic and with names for enduring objects, we can provide a provably adequate general theory of identity. The counterreply is saying, in effect, that there would be special problems about identity through time if we began with names for momentary objects. This may be so, but as it stands, it is irrelevant. The fact, if it is fact, that there are serious difficulties about defining identity through time in terms of the basic machinery of second-order logic supplemented with names of momentary objects, is, by itself, irrelevant to the question of whether one would have similar difficulties if one had available names for enduring objects.

One final counterreply seems possible.[21] Suppose that it could be shown that one ought not to begin with names for enduring objects. Suppose that it could be shown that on metaphysical or epistemological or logical grounds, there were reasons for treating these as dubious, and for requiring that one analyze them in terms of names of momentary objects. Then it would seem to follow that in proposing our theory, we have been engaged in the wrong type of program, and that our success is therefore irrelevant. This is an important suggestion, one that requires considerable discussion. Chapter Two will be devoted to it, and I will try to show there why this suggestion is ultimately in error.

TWO ✦ ENDURING AND NONENDURING OBJECTS

Chapter One defended the view that the identity of indiscernibles could serve as the basis of a general account of identity, one that provides necessary and sufficient conditions for the identity of any objects *a* and *b*, no matter of what type and no matter when they exist. It was shown at the end of that chapter, however, that this view presupposed that "identity" was being defined in a language that contained both the machinery of second-order logic and names for enduring objects. It was also suggested that if one was trying to define "identity" in a weaker language, a language that only contained names for merely momentary objects, the proposed definition of "identity" could not be offered. Given that this is so, it seems to suggest that our view is incomplete, that there remains the unsolved problem of specifying when momentary objects are parts of the same enduring objects.

I shall not, in this chapter, argue for the position that the proposed general theory of identity specifies when momentary objects are part of the same enduring object. As far as I can see, it does not; at least, it does not when the momentary objects are prior to the enduring objects. What I shall argue is that it is of little importance that it does not, for there is no particular reason to be concerned with its failure to do so. No doubt, many philosophers have felt that one should begin one's ontological scheme with merely momentary objects, and that one should construct, through a definition of "being part of the same object," enduring objects. If they were right, then our theory's failure to deal with this problem would be a fatal blow to it. I shall try to show, however, that there is no reason to agree with these philosophers, and that there is every reason to begin one's system with the enduring objects that we regularly encounter. If this is so, then the suggested gap left by our definition of "identity" will be of little importance.

It might seem that we have a stronger argument against this objection to our approach. Couldn't we follow Strawson in arguing that enduring objects (especially physical objects) must be ontologically prior to all other particulars? And if we could, then couldn't we conclude that an ontological scheme cannot begin with merely momentary objects, and that there is no problem left unsolved by our general theory of identity?

Although this is an attractive suggestion, I am afraid it must be rejected. As we shall show in the first section of this chapter, Strawson's argument fails at too many places. We shall, therefore, have to look in Section 2.2 at the program of beginning with merely momentary objects, and see whether there is anything to be said for it.

2.1 STRAWSON ON ONTOLOGICAL PRIORITY

Strawson claims to show that enduring objects (especially physical objects) are ontologically prior to all other particulars, including momentary objects.[1] What is meant by "ontological priority"? We shall say that an entity a is in a given person's ontology if and only if there is some object b identical with a such that that person believes that b exists and there is no object c identical with a such that that person believes that c does not exist. And we shall say that entities of type α are in a given person's ontology if and only if there is a type β identical with α such that that person believes that entities of type β exist and there is no type λ identical with α such that that person believes that entities of type λ do not exist. An entity a is ontologically prior to an entity b if and only if it would be a mistake for b to be in one's ontology when a is not in one's ontology (but not vice versa), while an entity type α is ontologically prior to an entity type β if and only if it would be a mistake for one to have α's in one's ontology when one does not have β's in one's ontology (but not vice versa). "It would be a mistake" is obviously vague, but that is precisely the reason for using it. We will be considering many different ways in which such a mistake might be committed, not merely the case in which the mistake is one of logical incoherency, so what is needed is some vague term that covers all of these ways.

It would be very helpful to know what is meant by "physical object" and "particular." But that is too long and difficult a matter to spell out now, so I will just say, as does Strawson, that things like chairs and tables, but not Caesar's crossing the Rubicon or my latest thought, are physical objects; and that all of these, but not the properties that they have, are particulars.

The argument that Strawson offers in sections 1–6 of chapter 1 seems to be divisible into two major sections. The first attempts to show that in order to introduce particulars into our ontology, we need to have a spatio-temporal framework in which these particulars are located. Its main steps are:

(1) A necessary condition for having particulars of type α in one's ontology is that one can refer to such particulars in such a way that a hearer will know, on the strength of one's referring act, which of these particulars one is referring to; that is, a necessary condition for having α's in one's ontology is that that one can identify α's.

(2) Since many particulars of any type α are not sensibly present to us at any given instance, we can only identify them by descriptions of them.

(3) Since any description in general terms can be satisfied by more than one particular, identifying descriptions must contain something else that can only be satisfied by a single particular.

(4) That something else is the spatiotemporal location of the particular being identified.

(5) So in order to have particulars of type α, for any α, in one's ontology, one must also possess a spatiotemporal framework in which these αs are located.

In response to this argument, I should like to claim that there are no reasons for believing that (1) and (3) are true; indeed, there are good reasons for believing that they are false.

Let us begin by having a look at (1). What reasons does Strawson advance for it?

That it should be possible to identify particulars of a given type seems to be a necessary condition of the inclusion of that type in our ontology. For what could we mean by claiming to acknowledge the existence of a class of particular things and to talk to each other about members of this class, if we qualified the claim by adding that it was in principle impossible for any one of us to make any other of us understand which member, or members, of this class he was at any time talking about? The qualification would seem to stultify the claim.[2]

Now there is something very strange about this argument. I grant that it would be meaningless (in the sense of pointless, the only sense that Strawson could have in mind here) for us to talk to each other about particulars if we couldn't let each other know which ones we were talking about. Perhaps it even follows from this that Strawson is right in saying that it would be meaningless for us to "acknowledge the existence of a class of particular things and to talk to each other about members of this class" if we couldn't let each other know which one we were talking about. But none of this is relevant to the claim that it would be meaningless for us simply to acknowledge the existence of this class of entities unless we could identify them, and this is, of course, the claim that Strawson is supposed to be defending. In other words, while there may be limitations from the point of view of communication about what we can do with entities that we cannot identify, it does not follow that there is anything wrong with, or pointless about, admitting them into one's ontology. The point of doing that might simply be that we want to have our ontology as complete as possible, that is, we want to have a complete list of all the types of entities that really do exist. And isn't that, after all, the traditional point of ontology anyway?

Strawson could always save his enterprise by confining himself to claims about ontological priority among entities that turn out to be identifiable. And I propose to consider the rest of his argument on the assumption that this limitation of scope has been imposed. The point of doing this is to enable us to see what else is wrong with the argument.

We come now to the very strange premise (3), which is really an argument that goes as follows: any description in general terms can be satisfied by more than one particular; therefore, identifying descriptions must contain something else that uniquely picks out the particular. It is clear that the soundness of this argument, and therefore the truth of premise (3), depends upon the truth of the missing assumption that an identifying description must be satisfiable by only one particular. But isn't this just false? After all, an identifying description is just a description used by one person that enables a second person, on the basis of the identifying description, to know which particular the first person is talking about. So if I say, "the lady in the red dress is John's mother," then "the lady in the red dress" is an identifying description if (as is often the case) you then know whom I am talking about, but "the lady in the red dress" is hardly a description satisfied by only one individual.

The peculiar thing about Strawson's use of premise (3) is that he is quite aware of this possibility of successful identifying references using descriptions that are satisfiable by more than one particular. He is even prepared to admit that in many of these cases we can know (or at least have some reasons for believing) that the identifying reference has been successful. Nevertheless, Strawson is not moved by this objection: "It does not explain the possibility of our having the conclusive reasons we may have. It yields no clues to the general structure of our thinking about identification."[3] What this remark suggests is that in those cases where we can make, and know that we have made, successful identifying references using only general terms, there is some other feature of the case that makes it possible. And in light of the second half of the remark and the rest of Strawson's arguments, it would seem that he believes that this other feature is the spatiotemporal location of the particular, the very thing that, when added to the general term description, yields a description that is uniquely satisfiable.

Strawson does not spell out his argument for these claims, but it seems to be the following: I am able to know that I have successfully identified the particular that I am referring to just because its spatial location at the time of the attempted identification makes it the best candidate for being the particular that the hearer will suppose that I am referring to. Thus, in many cases, since only one woman in a red dress is standing near us, you will understand that I am referring to her when I talk about the woman in a red dress. The general structure of nonostensive identification is thus based upon the spatiotemporal locatability of the particulars referred to, and it is just this that enables us to have in many cases conclusive or good reasons for supposing that the identification was successful.

But isn't it false that, in general, we can make and know that we have made successful identifying references only because of the spatiotemporal locatability of the objects we are referring to? If we both have seen only one woman in a red dress (perhaps we have been brought into a monastery as infants and have just left it), or if we have only seen one beautiful women, or if we are spies worrying about enemy agents and there is only one that is a woman wearing a red dress, or if . . . in all of these cases, and in as many others as our time and imagination allow us to think of, we can (and often do) make, and have conclusive or good reasons for believing that we have made, successful identifying references even without taking into account the spatiotemporal location of the objects referred to. So it looks as if Strawson's defense of step (3) is mistaken.

The second half of Strawson's argument attempts to show that the possession of a spatiotemporal framework required for the introduction of particulars presupposes the presence in one's ontology of a large and diverse group of physical objects. Its main steps are:

(6) The spatiotemporal framework is a single unified system, that is, any entity located in space (time) is spatially (temporally) related to any other such entity.

(7) In order for us to have such a framework, we must have in our ontology particulars that can be reidentified.

(8) Moreover, these particulars must be observable, three dimensional, and enduring; and collectively, they must have a good deal of diversity and richness of properties.

(9) Only physical objects possess all of these characteristics.

(10) Therefore, the possession of a spatiotemporal framework presupposes the presence of physical objects in one's ontology.

When (5) and (10) are combined, you get the desired final conclusion:

(11) In order to be ontologically committed to particulars of type α, one should already have in one's ontology physical objects.

In other words, physical objects are ontologically prior to αs.

Given the many difficulties that we have found in the argument for (5), the soundness of the argument for (10) would hardly justify (11). Nevertheless, as a background for our further investigations, we must have a good look at the move from (6) to (10), and a good way to begin is by considering the very strange step (6).

Step (6), as a description of the spatiotemporal framework that we do employ, may or may not be true. But even if it is true, need this be so? What necessity is there for the unity of the spatiotemporal framework? And should it be objected that this is part of what is meant by a "spatiotemporal" framework, then (although I would be very dubious about such a meaning claim) I would reraise my question as follows: is there any reason why we couldn't employ some nonunified framework to solve Strawson's problem about speaker-hearer identification?

But need (6) be necessarily true for the argument to proceed? Isn't it sufficient that it be true? This reply to my objection misses the point. After all, Strawson has argued [in steps (1)–(5)] for the need for some pervasive framework in which particulars are located, such that their location in this framework enables a speaker to identify them to his listeners. And he has also claimed that the spatiotemporal framework that we employ is just such a framework. Now the spatiotemporal framework that we employ has many interesting features, and Strawson would hardly want to claim (or, at least, he has offered us no reason for believing) that only a framework that possesses all of these features could meet the problem of identification. In step (6), however, he picks on one of these features, the unity of the spatiotemporal framework, and goes on to argue from this for the need for enduring physical objects in one's ontology in order to have the required pervasive framework. Then isn't it open for a critic to argue that we can have in our ontology identifiable particulars but no physical objects providing that the pervasive spatiotemporal framework employed is not a unified framework? Or, what really comes to the same thing, isn't it open for the critic to object that Strawson really needs the necessity of the identification-framework being a unified framework, and he has offered no argument for that claim.

Could one identify particulars to one's listener by reference to their location in such a nonunified framework? Why not? All that you need, even if you are worried about Strawson's problem of identification, is some additional fact about the particular that can be added to one's identifying reference so that it can be satisfied by only one particular. And all that is needed for that is a framework in which there cannot be two objects, having all their properties in common, which are in the same location in that framework. There seems to be no need for a unified framework, and any requirement of unity is therefore unwarranted.

We turn now to step (7). The argument that Strawson offers for it is that in order to be able to know about spatial relations over time, we have to be able to reidentify at least some spatial locations, and this involves reidentifying particulars. This last point seems plausible. After all, the locations have no intrinsic properties, so it looks as though we have to identify and reidentify them by reference to what is located in them.

Step (8) also seems satisfactory. The particulars have to endure for at least some time, or else we could not reidentify them. And unless they have a sufficiently rich and diverse set of qualities, how will we be able to tell that p_2 at t_2 is identical with p_1 at t_1 rather than with some other p at t_1? After all, as Hume already saw, it is qualitative resemblance that provides us with an epistemological basis for claims about numerical identity. Finally, they must be observable, or else we could not know enough about their properties so that we could settle questions about their identity.

Let us now look at step (9). Strawson says little about it in his original presentation of the argument, but he returns to its defense in the last section of chapter one. There are two types of objections that he considers there. One claims that we already have in our ordinary ontology other particulars besides physical objects whose reidentification could serve as the epistemological basis for a unified spatiotemporal framework. These include events and facts. The other claims that we might invent alternative ontologies (of process things, of fields, and so on) that do not even contain physical objects, and that Strawson's step (9) would be false for such ontologies.

Strawson has very little to say about the second type of

objection. He dismisses the objection from process-thing ontologies with the following: "I remarked earlier that I was concerned to investigate the relations of identifiability-dependence between the available major categories, the categories we actually possess; and the category of process-thing is one we neither have nor need."[4]

Leaving aside the last two words, this point about the scope of his own claim is unobjectionable. But it does suggest that Strawson has failed to consider the most fundamental question about identifiability dependence, viz. what are the features of physical objects that are necessary and sufficient for their playing the role that Strawson has assigned to them, and that would have to be satisfied by entities of a new category before they take over this role. Given the more limited task he set himself, all that Strawson had to find was a few necessary conditions that would rule out all our ordinary categories other than physical objects. The last two words seem to suggest something else. Perhaps Strawson is suggesting that considerations of new ontologies are pointless since our current ontology is perfectly adequate. This suggestion is most unfortunate. Even if we can (and do) make do with our current ontology, there may be other ontologies that are advantageous even for our normal needs, and even more so for new and specialized needs (like the needs of the advanced sciences). So the ontologist must consider alternative categories of particulars.

Strawson has much more to say about the first type of objection. Although he only discusses events, his points seem, to one who does not agree with Strawson's view that facts do not exist, equally applicable to facts, so we will consider them together. The first argument that he offers is a rather general one:

Suppose that αs are necessarily αs of βs (e.g., that births are necessarily births of animals). Then, although on a particular occasion, I may identify a particular α without identifying the β it is of, yet it would not in general be possible to identify αs unless it were in general possible to identify βs. For we could not speak of αs as we do speak of them, or have the concept we do have of αs, unless we spoke of βs; and we could not speak of βs unless it were in principle possible to identify a β.[5]

And since, says Strawson, events (and presumably facts) necessarily involve things, one has to be able to identify the latter in order to be able to identify the former, and one cannot use the former, therefore, as the basic entities for the purpose of identification.

There is something very suspicious about this argument. It certainly is not true that if there cannot be αs without βs, then we cannot have αs in our ontology without having βs in it as well. This might come about, for example, if one didn't have the concept of a β. Thus, in our case, one might have an ontology of events without things if one had simple and unanalyzable concepts of certain events out of which other more complicated events were constructable. To be sure, the possessor of such an ontological scheme might thereby be missing certain information (about the composition of his simple events), but that doesn't rule out such an ontological scheme. So it looks as though the general argument is simply mistaken.

Strawson might reply that we have missed the point of "as we speak of them" and "we do have" in the argument. They are there precisely to meet our objection. After all, our concept of an event (or a fact) contains the idea that there are things involved in these events (or facts), and for our ontology, then, the objection is irrelevant. This reply would, of course, move the event and fact objection into the same class as the process-thing objection, and we need not repeat here our dissatisfaction with Strawson's treatment of that. We should only note that there is very little left in the scope of his claim.

Strawson has another, and according to him a more serious, reply to the event objection. He claims that there is no relatively permanent series of well spread out events that satisfy the following conditions: (*i*) one member can always be directly identified, and (*ii*) all other members can be identified by their position in the series. Consequently, there is no series of events whose members are identifiable independently of the identification of other types of particulars (like physical objects) that we can use as the basis for identifying other particulars.

Although Strawson has much to say about the difficulty of constructing such a series of events, he does not offer much evidence in support of his claim. He has, of course, little difficulty in showing that it is true for a series of flashes and bangs. After all, we often don't have even one flash or bang that is directly locatable. He realizes that more complicated sequences, involving different types of events, are possible, and yet he doesn't even attempt to show that they would have similar shortcomings. So we must conclude that Strawson has not proven his point.

Three conclusions seem to emerge from our examination of Strawson's argument:

(a)   There is serious doubt as to whether there is a problem about identification that requires as part of its solution the acceptance of a spatiotemporal framework. But even if this problem exists, this has no ontological significance, since there is no connection between questions of ontological commitment and questions of identification.

(b)   One of the key steps in Strawson's argument is the assumption of the necessary unity of the spatiotemporal framework, and the arguments advanced by Strawson fail to show its necessity for the purpose of identification.

(c)   Physical objects seem to be only one of many enduring particulars that could serve as basic particulars for identification. Is there any reason for preferring them? Strawson fails to advance any convincing reasons.

We need not consider problem (c) any further since it only relates to the question of whether physical objects are prior to other enduring objects, a question of no concern to us now. All that we have to note is that problems (a) and (b) completely undercut Strawson's argument for the ontological priority of enduring objects. We must, therefore, look for other reasons for rejecting the program of beginning with momentary objects.

2.2 THE CONSTRUCTIONIST PROGRAM

Perhaps it would be best to begin with a review of the program of beginning with merely momentary objects and constructing permanent objects out of them, to which we shall refer as the constructionist program. We shall take as an example of this program Carnap's classic *Der Logische Aufbau der Welt*, first published in 1928.[6] Our concern is, of course, with the basic ideas behind the program, and not with its detailed implementation. We shall show below that the same basic arguments are offered by more recent authors such as John Perry.

Carnap explained that the goal of his constructionist program was to show how all of our concepts can be derived from a few basic concepts. An additional, and consequential, goal was to show that there could be one science which studied all that existed, the science of the objects corresponding to the basic concepts.

What did Carnap mean by "derive," and what did he mean by a "basic concept"? Carnap made it clear that in order to derive a concept A from some more basic concepts $B, C, \ldots$, all statements about A must be translatable into statements about $B, C \ldots$. This is a requirement that he (and many other constructionists) later weakened. He also made it clear that the basic concepts are simply those that are not derived from any other concepts. In short, then, Carnap felt that his program would succeed if he could show how to translate all meaningful statements into statements about his basic concepts.

Carnap chose as the most important of his basic concepts that of the instantaneous total experience. He might have chosen some more traditional momentary candidates like momentary physical objects or separate sense-data, but under the influence of classical empiricism he rejected the former as not being epistemologically basic, and under the influence of Gestalt psychology he rejected the latter as not being psychologically basic. For Carnap, then, the constructionist program consisted in showing how all statements can be translated into statements about instantaneous total experiences. Carnap carried out this program in a number of steps. There is one that is of crucial importance for us. At a certain point in his construction, he reached the question of constructing enduring world-lines (and then enduring visual things) out of world-points (momentary nonsubjective objects). To do this, Carnap introduced the relation of genidentity, the relation that holds between world-points if they are part of an enduring world-line. This is the relation with which our general account of identity does not deal, and it is this lack of completeness whose importance we are trying to assess.

There are those who have held that the main interest in starting with instantaneous objects is merely to see what can be constructed starting with them, but that there is no reason to ascribe any special significance to the constructionist program. Goodman expressed such a viewpoint in defending Carnap's choice of a phenomenal base:

> I am ready to maintain that the value of efforts to construct a system on a phenomenalistic or any other narrow basis is very little affected by whether or not the system can be completed. . . . Only by positive efforts with severely restricted means can we make any progress in construction; only so can we discern the exact limitations of a basis and the exact supplementation needed.[7]

This attitude implies that the inability of our approach to define genidentity for the constructionist program is not a serious objection to it; our approach would be seriously incomplete only if there is some reason for ascribing special importance to the constructionist program (for example, if there was something inappropriate in starting with enduring objects).

Carnap's own approach when he wrote the *Aufbau* was very different. He felt that starting with momentary total experiences was the appropriate procedure because it reflected their epistemological primacy:

> The system form which we want to give to our outline of the constructional system is characterized by the fact that it not only attempts to exhibit, as any system form, the order of objects relative to their reducibility, but that it also attempts to show their order relative to epistemic primacy. An object (or an object type) is called epistemically primary relative to another one, which we call epistemically secondary, if the second one is recognized through the mediation of the first and thus presupposes, for its recognition, the recognition of the first. [8]

This account clearly implies that the inability of our approach to define genidentity for the constructionist program is a major problem for our approach. If certain constructions are required by our epistemological situation, then any satisfactory theory of identity must surely provide the identity-aspects of those constructions.

What exactly is Carnap's argument? We can distinguish two related reconstructions of it:

(I) What we directly experience are momentary objects (in particular, momentary total experiences). The existence of anything else has to be inferred from the existence of these directly experienced momentary objects. This is possible only if everything else is constructible out of these directly experienced momentary objects. This is why the implementation of the constructionist program is such an important metaphysical task.

(II) The first objects of our knowledge are momentary objects (in particular, momentary total experiences). We later learn by inference of the existence of other objects. This process of learning is possible only because these other objects can be constructed out of the momentary objects.

This is why the implementation of the constructionist program is such an important metaphysical task.

There is little to say in behalf of argument (I). Its crucial first premise, that momentary objects are the objects of our direct experience, seems particularly insupportable in light of the collapse of sense-data theories (the type of theories by which Carnap, no doubt, was influenced, although that influence was sufficiently mediated by Gestalt theory so that Carnap insisted that the basic objects are the total momentary experiences). Probably the best way to try to support that premise today (a way that has seemed to lie behind many remarks made to me when I have discussed these issues) would be to avoid the sense-data approach, and to offset the fact that we certainly seem to directly experience such enduring objects as chairs, trees and people by arguing as follows:

(a) We can only directly experience what exists at the time of the act of experiencing it.

(b) Enduring objects exist both before and after the acts of experiencing them.

(c) We can only directly experience momentary objects.

But even this argument won't do. Its crucial premise (a) is ambiguous between

(a′) we can only directly experience something which exists, among other times, at the time of the act of experiencing it;

and

(a″) we can only directly experience something which exists only at the time of the act of experiencing it.

Premise (a′), which has some plausibility (although the time-gap problem raises doubts about it as well), does not, even when supplemented by (b), entail (c). Premise (a″)

does, but what reason is there for believing it? Whatever plausibility there may be in claiming that the object experienced must exist at the time at which it is experienced does not extend to claiming that it can only exist then. So even the best argument for (I)'s first premise fails.

There is another premise in (I) that deserves some further comment. It is the assumption that the inference from the momentary to the enduring would be possible only if the enduring were constructable out of the momentary. Again, this is an assumption in favor of which there is little to say. It simply fails to recognize that one might infer (nondeductively, of course) the existence of B from the existence of A even if B is not constructable out of A.

In short, then, argument (I) is extremely weak. Let us now look at argument (II). Its crucial first premise, that the first objects of our knowledge are momentary objects, seems as objectionable as (I)'s first premise. But there is actually a way of reading argument (II) that makes it somewhat more plausible. It runs as follows:

(a)   Even if the objects that are the first objects of our knowledge really are enduring objects, we first believe of them that they are momentary objects. At least this much must be granted in light of the work of Piaget and his associates.

(b)   At a later stage, we infer from various features of our experience that these objects really are enduring objects. In doing so, we construct the idea of an enduring object out of our idea of a momentary object with the aid of a genidentity relation.

(c)   The constructionist program has metaphysical significance just because it recaptures this important psychological process.

The main problem with this somewhat more plausible argument is that it, like all the arguments we have considered, presupposes that learning and inference can take place only if the constructionist program can be carried out. But why should this presupposition be granted? When various constancies in our experience are noted, we accept the idea of enduring objects as a way of accounting for them. This process (which bears a resemblance to the inference to the best explanation) in no way requires the possibility of constructing enduring objects out of momentary objects.

It might be thought that Carnap's epistemological arguments have been superseded by more sophisticated arguments on behalf of the constructionist program. I think not. Without exhaustively reviewing the recent literature, I would at least like to illustrate this point by referring to a much-discussed and rightly much-admired recent article by John Perry. Perry, in that article, is trying to defend a modified version of Grice's theory of personal identity, a theory that constructs persons out of total temporary states. He says the following about the motivation for such a program:

> The logical constructor attempts to analyze sentences about objects of some category into sentences about objects of some other category. . . . At the bottom of the structure are sentences with a favored epistemological status, as, for example, that they can be directly known, because the objects they are about can be directly inspected. Through analysis, this favored status, or at least some status more favorable than was originally apparent, is transmitted up the structure to the analyzed sentences. Talk about persons might have seemed to involve us in talk about pure egos, or substances of some other obscure sort, but when we see that talk of persons is, really, just talk of total temporary states and ultimately, of experiences, our knowledge is revealed as more secure than it seemed.[9]

We see Perry arguing here along the lines of argument (I). He seems to be just assuming that talk about enduring persons cannot be primitive because such objects, unlike momentary experiences, cannot be directly experienced. And we have seen no reason to believe this. There is, to be sure, the extra suggestion that persons are pure egos which cannot be experienced. But surely there is no reason to accept that extra claim; put otherwise, those who take enduring objects like persons as primitive don't have to think about them in these obscure ways.

Let us see where we now stand. We have seen that, contra Strawson, momentary particulars are not necessarily dependent upon enduring particulars. In that way, there is nothing objectionable in the idea of beginning one's ontology with momentary objects. At the same time, we have seen that neither epistemology nor psychology requires the executability of the constructionist program. Moreover, whatever may be the case in our infancy, the objects of our concern as adults are enduring objects, and it is they that we encounter both in perception and thought. I conclude, therefore, that while we have not solved the problem of genidentity for the constructionist, this is not a fundamental gap in our theory of identity, a theory that is rightfully concerned with the identity of enduring objects.

THREE ✦ IMPLICATIONS

The first two chapters have defended an approach to the theory of identity that can be summarized as follows: the enduring objects that we perceive and of which we think can and should be taken as fundamental in an ontology. For all such objects, indiscernibility (understood in a sufficiently broad fashion) is both a necessary and sufficient condition for identity. This is a perfectly general condition for identity, and involves no conditions that vary according to the type of object involved.

This approach has significant implications for a variety of philosophical claims involving identity. This chapter will consider a variety of these implications.

3.1 PHYSICAL OBJECTS AND SPATIOTEMPORAL CONTINUITY

Philosophers have normally assumed that spatiotemporal continuity is a necessary and sufficient condition for the identity of physical objects. In fact, the only serious question that has been raised about this assumption relates to the exact meaning of that continuity. Our approach, however, questions the very validity of this assumption.

Why does it do so? Well, there doesn't seem to be any justification for the claim that spatiotemporal continuity is a necessary condition for physical objects satisfying the requirement of indiscernibility, which is sufficient for their identity. It would seem, therefore, that the claim that spatiotemporal continuity is a necessary condition for the identity of physical objects is, at best, a hypothesis whose justification is very unclear. Similarly, there doesn't seem to be any justification for the claim that spatiotemporal continuity is a sufficient condition for physical objects satisfying the requirement of indiscernibility, which is necessary for their identity. It would seem, therefore, that the claim that spatiotemporal continuity is a sufficient condition for the identity of physical objects is, at best, a hypothesis whose justification is very unclear.

Figures 1 and 2 might make this point clearer. Figure 1 helps show why our approach suggests that spatiotemporal

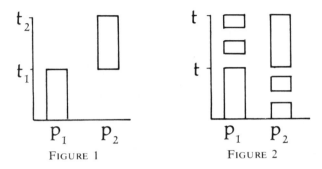

FIGURE 1   FIGURE 2

continuity is not necessary for the identity of physical objects. It pictures an object o's history. Up to and including t_1, object o was in place p_1. At all times after t_1, object o is in place p_2 at some distance from p_1. At all times, o has the same properties as itself. Let o be a and b. Then, here we have a case of objects a and b that satisfy the condition of indiscernibility and are identical, but that do not satisfy the condition of spatiotemporal continuity. Figure 2 helps show why our approach suggests that spatiotemporal continuity is not sufficient for the identity of physical objects. Up to and including t_1, object o_1 (represented by the solid line) is in p_1, and the different object o_2 (represented by the broken line) is in p_2. At all times after t_1, o_2 is in p_1, while o_1 is in p_2. Let a be o_1 at t_1, and let b be o_2 after t_1. Then a is spatiotemporally continuous with b, and yet they are discernible and not therefore identical. So, spatiotemporal continuity is not apparently sufficient for the identity of physical objects.

The possibilities that are portrayed in these pictoral representations might, of course, be advanced independently of our approach as objections to the necessity or sufficiency of spatiotemporal continuity. Advanced that way, however, they have little force. What, it could be objected, does it mean to say that it is o in p_1 up to t_1 and in p_2 thereafter? Our approach answers that question. It means that the object in p_2 after t_1 has, at all times, the same properties had, at that time, by the object occupying p_1 up to and including t_1. Our theory, therefore, provides the content for these claims about counterexamples to the continuity condition.

In discussing these examples, I have said that, combined with our account of identity, they suggest that spatiotemporal continuity is neither necessary nor sufficient for the identity of physical objects. I have not said that they prove this, primarily because I could imagine doubt about these examples. How, after all, do we know that the description of these examples are coherent? Perhaps, independently of the definition of "identity," there are conceptual impossibilities with the idea of discontinuous motion presupposed in these examples, difficulties that rule out these examples and that at least entail the necessity of spatiotemporal continuity (and perhaps even entail the sufficiency of that continuity) for the identity of physical objects?

It is hard to meet these doubts, for it is hard to prove the nonexistence of independent conceptual difficulties with the idea of discontinuous motion. There are, nevertheless, a number of further points that can be made to buttress our suggestion that continuity is neither required nor sufficient for the identity of physical objects.

(a) The identity of the subatomic particles that make up physical objects does not seem to involve spatiotemporal continuity. To begin with, as Hanson has argued, the movement of an electron to a wider orbit involves discontinuous motion.[1] So we have here a case of an electron at t_1 identical with an electron at t_2 (in a wider orbit), and yet not spatiotemporally continuous with that earlier electron. Second, it has been widely suggested that, in the case of photon-electron scattering, electrons move backwards in time and then forwards again, thus producing a case of discontinuous motion (at least on the ordinary accounts of continuity). We would again have here a case of electron-identity not involving spatiotemporal continuity.

(b) We can offer a clearly coherent description of observations that seem most naturally to suggest that they be interpreted as being cases of the type depicted in Figure 1 or Figure 2. Therefore, the defender of the view that there are independent conceptual bars to discontinuous motion is forced to make the ad hoc move that such observations would have, of necessity, to be described otherwise. The observations suggesting Figure 1 are the following: up to and including t_1, we observe a very strange-looking object in place p_1. In light of the very unusual properties of this object, there is good reason to believe that it is the only such object in existence (or, at least, in the reasonably near vicinity). Now there is a place p_2 which is some distance from p_1, and there is a mechanism that signals when an object approaches near p_2 from any direction (but stops when the object reaches p_2). Just after t_1, we look at p_1 and observe that the strange-looking object is not there, and we also observe that an object exactly like it is now at p_2. But the mechanism has not signaled the approach of an object to p_2. In such a case (providing that we exclude many other possibilities), it might become plausible to say, although difficult to explain, that the object which used to be in p_1 is now in p_2, but did not traverse a continuous path from p_1 to p_2. The observations suggesting Figure 2 are the following: up to and including t_1, we observe a very strange-looking object at p_1, and a very different, but also very strange-looking object at p_2, which is some distance from p_1. In light of the very unusual properties of both of these objects, there are good reasons to believe that they are the only such objects in existence (or, at least, in the reasonably near vicinity). There are mechanisms that signal when an object approaches near p_1 or near p_2 from any direction (but stop when the object reaches p_1 or p_2). Now just after t_1, we observe in p_2 an object just like the strange-looking object that used to be in p_1 (and we do not observe one like it in p_1) and we observe in p_1 an object just like the strange-looking object that used to be in p_2 (and we do not observe one like it in p_2). But the mechanisms have not signaled the approach of an object to either p_1 or p_2. In such a case (providing that we exclude many other possibilities), it might become plausible to say, although difficult to explain, that the object which used to be in p_1 is now in p_2 and the object which used to be in p_2 is now in p_1, but neither traversed a continuous path from p_1 to p_2. While not conclusive, it seems to me that these considerations count heavily against the claim that spatiotemporal continuity is necessarily connected with identity on some grounds independent of the definition of "identity."

In saying all of this, I am not, of course, denying the usefulness of spatiotemporal continuity in establishing that some physical object a is identical with some physical object b. I am only arguing that there is no conceptual necessary connection between the two, and that our ability to use continuity as evidence for identity is based upon our learning that physical objects normally move in a continuous fashion.

I know of only one major challenge to our claim of the possibility of discontinuous motion, that offered by Professor Coburn.[2] Professor Coburn has an argument, independent of the definition of "identity," for the impossibility of discontinuous motion and for the necessity of spatiotemporal continuity for the identity of physical objects. It runs as follows:

> Suppose that there could be a case of a material object's exhibiting spatial discontinuity. . . . Then it would seem that there could (logically) be three qualitatively indistinguishable marbles each of which undergoes a discontinuous translation in space at the same instant [Coburn refers to the three before the translation as the left-hand marbles, and as a, b, and c, and the three after as the right-hand marbles, and as d, e, and f]. . . . But in order for this situation to be logically possible, it

must make sense to say, for example, that $a = d$ and that $a \neq d$. . . . That it does, however, this line of thought continues, is very doubtful. For given the qualitative indistinguishability of the marbles involved, there seems to be no way of pairing the left-hand marbles with the right ones which has more to commend it than has any alternative way of pairing them. But if nothing whatever could justify identifying a with d (say) as opposed to e or f, then it does not make clear sense to maintain that each left-hand marble is identical with one of the right-hand marbles.[3]

This statement of the argument won't do, for we can give clear sense to the claim that $a = d$ as opposed to e and f, even if, because of the indistinguishability of the marbles, we cannot tell that it is d with which a is identical. To say that $a = d$ and not e or f is to say, among other things, that, at the earlier time, d was where a was while, at that time, e and f were elsewhere. In other words, indiscernibility, understood in our broad sense, can give content to the identity claims whose truth we cannot ascertain and whose meaningfulness Coburn would then challenge.

Coburn, in another passage, shifts the argument and puts it this way:

For in the marble case, unlike these others, there is nothing more to know that is relevant to the question whether $a = d$. But this is tantamount to saying that we can form no conception of what it would be for anyone to know that $a = d$. However, the notion that an intelligible statement should be a garden variety empirical one, and yet that we should be able to form no conception of what it would be for anyone to know that it is true (or false) is most dubious.[4]

Here, the argument has switched clearly toward a verificationist bent. It is also clear, however, that Coburn is (very wisely) not willing to rest his argument on some dubious verifiability principle. The real support of the argument is the notion of a "garden variety" empirical statement, for his claim seems to be that only they must be such that we have a conception of what it would be to know their truth value.

What is a "garden variety empirical statement"? Is there any reason to accept a quasi-verificationist principle involving them? Is the claim that marble a = marble d in the case of a discontinuous motion a "garden variety empirical statement"? Coburn says absolutely nothing about these questions, and I do not myself see how to round out his argument. I shall, therefore, have to conclude tentatively that, given our account of identity, we can make sense of identity across discontinuous motion, and that we should tentatively reject the claim that spatiotemporal continuity is necessary for the identity of physical objects.

3.2 THE CONDITIONS OF PERSONAL IDENTITY

The theory that we have presented as a general account of the identity of enduring objects also provides an account of the conditions for it being the case that person p_1 is identical with person p_2. In this section, I will consider the implications of that account for the role of bodily continuity and continuity of memory and personality in the theory of personal identity, and for the resolution of the many problem cases involving personal identity.

Many philosophers have subscribed to one or the other of the following claims concerning personal identity:

1. *Claim of bodily continuity*—p_1 at t_1 is identical with p_2 at t_2 just in case p_1's body at t_1, b_1, is identical with p_2's body at t_2, b_2, and this is so just in case b_1 is spatiotemporally continuous with b_2.
2. *Claim of memory continuity*—p_1 at t_1 is identical with p_2 at t_2 just in case p_2's memories and character traits at t_2 are directly or indirectly continuous with p_1's memories and character traits at t_1.

Our approach questions both of these claims.

Why does it do so? Well, there seems to be no justification for the claim that b_1's being continuous with b_2 or p_1's memories and character traits being continuous with p_2's is necessary for p_1 and p_2 having, at each moment, all of their properties in common (so that they are identical on our account). It would seem, therefore, that the claim that bodily continuity or memory continuity is a necessary condition for the identity of persons is, at best, a hypothesis whose justification is very unclear. Similarly, there doesn't seem to be any justification for the claim that b_1's spatiotemporal continuity with b_2 or p_1's continuity of memory and experience with p_2 is sufficient for p_1 and p_2 having all of their properties in common at each moment of time (which is, on our account, necessary for their identity). It would seem, therefore, that the claim that bodily continuity or continuity of memory is sufficient for the identity of persons is, at best, a hypothesis whose justification is very unclear.

This last point can be made clearer by use of some of the standard problem cases involving personal identity.[5] Consider, for example, the actual case of a person who suffers a traumatic accident as a result of which he remembers little of his past and is radically transformed in his character. This problem case, often advanced by opponents of the claim of memory continuity, is an example of a case in which there is a p_1 before the accident and a p_2 after the accident who are identical just because they have all of their properties in common but who do not satisfy the condition of memory continuity. Or consider the hypothetical case of a person who wakes up one morning to find himself in a very different body far removed from the one he previously occupied. This problem case, often advanced by opponents of the claim of bodily continuity, is an example of a case in which there is a p_1 before the transformation and a p_2 afterwards who are identical just because they have all of their properties in common, but who do not satisfy the condition of bodily continuity. Similar examples can be constructed to cast doubt upon the claim that either bodily continuity or memory continuity is sufficient for identity.

These problem cases have, of course, been advanced independently of our approach as objections to the necessity of bodily or memory continuity. Indeed, one of the perplexing features about personal identity is just this fact that there seem to be pervasive counterexamples to all proposed conditions. What our approach does, however, is to lend extra force to these objections. After all, advanced independently of our approach, these counterexamples are far less forceful. What, it could be objected, does it mean in these cases to say that it's the same person before and after the accident or the transformation? Our approach answers that question. It means that p_1 and p_2 have, at all times, the same properties. Our approach provides then the content for the claims involved in these counterexamples.

Notice that the acceptance of these counterexamples leads to a relatively strong result. It seems clear, given our definition of "identity," that neither the claim of bodily continuity nor the claim of memory continuity follows from the definition of "identity." These counterexamples, given content by our definition of identity, also strongly suggest that there are no independent conceptual bases for these continuity claims. If they are true, they are true merely as a matter of fact.

I would like to add one additional remark about the counterexample to the claim about the necessity of memory continuity for personal identity. Recent years have seen the revival of memory theories of personal identity. Perhaps the most prominent version of such theories is the one advocated by John Perry, which places special emphasis upon the causal processes by which the person at t_2 remembers experiences had by the person at t_1.[6] I want to leave aside for now the question as to whether this appeal to causal processes, which has become so popular in so many areas of philosophy, is really helpful. All I want to point out for now is that it seems of little help in defending against the classical counterexamples. For example, the victim of the traumatic accident still shows that the necessity portion of the appropriately modified memory-claim is false.

There is no doubt, of course, that both bodily continuity and continuity of memory play a prominent role in our everyday identification of some p_2 at t_2 with some p_1 at t_1. It seems likely that it is this prominent role that has led many philosophers mistakenly to advance the above-mentioned claims. What, then, is this role? I believe that it is a merely evidentiary role, and one based upon experience.

The suggestion I should like to advance is this: the spatiotemporal continuity of b_2 with b_1 is merely evidence for the identity of p_2 with p_1, and the direct or indirect continuity of p_2's memories and character traits with p_1's memories and character traits is also merely evidence for the identity of p_2 with p_1. And they are evidence, not because of some necessary and a priori truth, but just because we have learned (in a nonenumerative fashion) from our experiences that people do not change their bodies (which move in a spatiotemporally continuous fashion), and that memories and character traits change in a more or less continuous fashion.

Professor Swinburne has recently advocated a similar position. He says:

> Wherein does the identity of persons consist? The identity does not consist solely in the continuity of one or more observable characteristics, for empiricist theories took all of these into account. . . . The only alternative is to say that personal identity is something ultimate. It is unanalyzable into conjunctions or disjunctions of other observable properties. Bodily continuity, continuity of memory and character, are however the only evidence we have of its presence; it is observable only by observing these.[7]

There are, however, some major differences between our positions.

Swinburne and I agree that personal identity is not some observable property or some conjunction or disjunction of observable properties. But he goes on to infer from this that "the only alternative" is that personal identity is an indefin-

able and ultimate concept. I feel that there is an other and
better alternative, the impredicative definition of personal
identity, a definition that applies equally well to all other
types of identity involving enduring objects.

Our other differences have to do with continuities as evidence for personal identity. Swinburne says, in the above-
quoted passage, that it is the only evidence. And in a later
passage, he adds:

> That evidence of continuity of body, memory, and
> character is evidence of personal identity cannot of
> course be something established by enumerative induc-
> tion. . . . Although it might in theory be established by
> some more complex form of inductive inference that the
> former is evidence of the latter, this is in fact, I suspect,
> either an analytic truth or some basic principle which
> we assume to be intuitively obvious.[8]

A number of comments seem to be in order here: (a) it
seems just wrong to say that these continuities are the only
evidence we have of personal identity. Consider the many
ways in which we can reidentify people (fingerprints, identification papers that they carry, special clothing that they
wear, knowledge of identifying formulas, and so on). Unless
"continuity of body, memory, and character" is used so
broadly as to exclude nothing except discontinuities, Swinburne's claim won't do; (b) most importantly, Swinburne's
claim that it is a more than empirical truth that these continuities are evidence for identity is very questionable. He
himself recognizes that there are ways in which this evidentiary relation could be established in an inductive (although
nonenumerative) fashion. Moreover, it seems to be an empirical question as to whether this evidentiary relation
exists. Swinburne himself admits that it is logically possible
that the relevant continuities be present without personal
identity being present, and vice versa. And if that is logically
possible, then isn't it logically possible that this happen on
many occasions? And if so, wouldn't that destroy the
evidentiary relation? And if so, doesn't that mean that the

existence of the evidentiary relation must be empirically ascertained by some nonenumerative form of induction?

These last remarks deserve some further comment. It still
seems to be popular in certain circles to insist upon the
possibility of evidentiary relations not involving logical en-
tailments whose existence is known nonempirically. It
seems to me that maintaining this view requires one to make
either of two extremely implausible moves: (a) while it is
logically possible that the evidence-phenomena and the phenomena evidenced occur independently, it is not logically
possible that they do so regularly, or (b) even if they regularly occur independently of each other, the occurrence of at
least one is still evidence for the occurrence of the other. I
suggest that it is far more reasonable to drop the idea of
these special evidentiary relations.

We have so far discussed the implications of our approach
to identity for the role of bodily continuity and continuity of
memory and personality in the theory of personal identity.
Before turning to its implications for the problem cases, one
final remark is in order.

Many people believe that they will survive their death,
that there will be some person p_n who exists after they have
died who is identical with them. This belief comes in two
versions, one (related to the doctrine of the resurrection of
the body) which claims that that person is embodied, and
one (related to the doctrine of the immortality of the soul)
which claims that that person is a disembodied person. But
there are philosophers who claim that a proper understanding of the concept of personal identity would show that those
beliefs are incoherent, would show that p_n could not be identical with the earlier embodied person who died.[9] The basis
of their claim is the claim of bodily continuity. Given that
claim, it follows immediately that no disembodied person
can be identical with any embodied person (and that, therefore, the second version of the belief in survival and the
doctrine of the immortality of the soul are incoherent). It
also follows (unless one wants to claim that p_n's body is
continuous with the body of the original person before his

death) that even the embodied p_n could not be identical with the original person who died (and that, therefore, the first version of the belief in survival and the doctrine of the resurrection of the body are incoherent). From the perspective of the theory of identity that we have presented, it would seem that this challenge to the coherency of these beliefs is mistaken. It is based upon the claim of bodily continuity, a claim that is not necessarily true. From our perspective, all that is required for p_n to be identical with the original person is that they have all of their properties in common. And there seems to be nothing in the supposition that the original person died that would rule out p_n and the original person having all of their properties in common. So, from the perspective of our theory, the concept of personal identity poses no conceptual problems for the beliefs in survival.

Let us turn to the problem cases that have so perplexed writers on the topic of personal identity. Consider first the following "switching case": at time t_{1-2} there is a person p_1 with a body b_1 and a set of memories and character traits m_1, and a person p_2 ($\neq p_1$) with a body b_2 ($\neq b_1$) and a set of memories and character traits m_2 ($\neq m_1$), and at time t_{3-4}, there is a person p_3 with a body b_3 and a set of memories and character traits m_3, and a person p_4 ($\neq p_3$) with a body b_4 ($\neq b_3$) and a set of memories and character traits m_4 ($\neq m_3$). The trouble arises when b_1 is spatiotemporally continuous with b_3 and not with b_4, and b_2 is spatiotemporally continuous with b_4 and not b_3 (leading us to identify p_1 with p_3 and p_2 with p_4), while m_4 is continuous with m_1 and not m_2, and m_3 is continuous with m_2 and not m_1 (leading us to identify p_1 with p_4 and p_2 with p_3). What then are we to say about p_1, p_2, p_3, and p_4? Traditionally, philosophers have looked at such cases as crucial cases testing the merits of two competing definitions of personal identity (the definition based upon the claim of bodily continuity and the definition based upon the claim of memory continuity). The trouble with such a test, however, is that we have no clear intuitions about what to say about such cases, so the test is not a very good one.

From our new perspective, however, the whole situation

looks very different. Persons p_3 and p_4 are identical with those persons, if any, existing at t_{1-2} with which they have all of their properties in common. Normally, the continuity of b_3 with b_1 and not b_2, and the continuity of b_4 with b_2 and not b_1 would indicate that $p_3 = p_1$ and $p_4 = p_2$. And normally, the continuity of m_4 with m_1 and not m_2, and m_3 with m_2 and not m_1 would indicate that $p_4 = p_1$ and $p_3 = p_2$. But here, at least one of these indicators has led us astray, and our puzzlement is about which one it is. On our account, then, this puzzlement is an example of a very general type of phenomenon, the puzzlement that arises when two generally reliable indicators lead to conflicting results. More importantly, our account also explains how such puzzlements are to be resolved. We shall adopt in this case, as in all other such cases, the account that best gives us a unified description and explanation of what has occurred. We may suppose that $p_1 = p_3$ and $p_2 = p_4$ and that we have here a case of memory transference; we may suppose that $p_1 = p_4$ and $p_2 = p_3$ and we have here a case of body switching; we may . . . Which move we make will be determined by considerations of theoretical simplicity and not by any considerations having to do with the meaning of "identity." Our theory, then, makes it clear why the problem is puzzling and how it would be resolved.

Before leaving our consideration of this case, it is helpful to contrast it with some remarks that Professor Flew has made about such cases:

> . . . since our ordinary language, and the concepts of ordinary language, have been evolved or introduced to deal with the situations which are ordinarily met with, and not with the extraordinary, we may reasonably expect some failures of adaptation when new and unexpected situations arise. . . . The old conceptual machinery breaks down. The old terminological tools fail to cope with the new tasks. These breakdowns are different from the cases in which indecision arises from the vagueness of a term. . . . It is this open texture

much more than any actual vagueness in use which prevents the definition of "person."[10]

It seems to me that Professor Flew has missed the point. If our account is correct, then although we face a crisis if and when such a case arises, the crisis is a scientific one (figuring out which indicator of identity has gone wrong and why) and not a conceptual crisis arising from the open texture of "identity."

Philosophers have, in recent years, devoted considerable attention to a problem that was first discussed by Bernard Williams.[11] This is the so-called "splitting problem." The following is the most general version of that problem: suppose that p_1 at t_1 is identical with p_2 at t_2 just in case relation R holds between them. Imagine now a case in which at time t_{2-3} there are two different people p_2 and p_3, and both $p_2 \ R \ p_1$ and $p_3 \ R \ p_1$. Then they are both identical with p_1 and therefore with each other, and we have, therefore, encountered a contradiction. As an example of this problem, consider the following argument offered by Williams against continuity of memory and character as a sufficient condition for identity:

> Suppose a person A to undergo a sudden change, and to acquire a character exactly like that of some person known to have lived in the past, B. Suppose him further to make sincere memory claims which entirely fit the life of B. We might think these conditions sufficient for us to identify A (as he now is) with B. But they are not. For another contemporary person, C, might undergo an exactly similar change at the same time as A, and if the conditions were sufficient to say that A = B, they would be sufficient to say that C = B as well. But it cannot be the case both that A = B and C = B, for, were it so, it would follow that A = C, which is absurd.[12]

The same sort of problem would arise if we asserted that bodily continuity is sufficient for the identity of persons, since we can envisage a case in which our body, like the amoeba's, splits in half.

There are many possible ways of dealing with this problem:

(a) We can say that p_2 is identical with p_1 just in case only p_2 bears at t_2 the relation R to p_1. Therefore, in the envisaged case, p_1 is identical with neither p_2 nor p_3, and has in fact gone out of existence (alternatively, it has split into two parts, neither of which is identical with the original whole).

(b) We can keep our definition of identity as it is, identify p_2 with p_1 and p_3 with p_1, avoid the contradiction by denying the transitivity of identity and therefore by not allowing the inference to $p_2 = p_3$.

(c) We can agree that, before the split, $p_1 = p_2 = p_3$ was true and that, since the split, "$p_2 \neq p_3$" is true. We would deny, however, any truth-value to statements after the split involving "p_1" on the grounds that it no longer uniquely names (the intuitive idea behind this is, of course, that identity is a time-relative relation).

(d) We can deny the legitimacy of the concept of identity by insisting that this paradox shows that the concept of a one-to-one identity relation is incoherent.

Each of these has been adopted by some author. Bernard Williams has advocated a version of (a),[13] Arthur Prior has suggested (b),[14] John Perry has suggested (c),[15] and Derek Parfit has forcefully argued for (d).[16]

What is essential for the generation of this problem is, of course, the possibility of there being two different entities that bear the relation R to p_1. Solution (a) recognizes that this is the root of the problem, and tries to rule it out. Unfortunately, it does so in an ad hoc fashion, by simply adding the requirement that p_2 must be the only person at t_2 bearing R to p_1. Moreover, it makes the definition of "identity" circular, since "only" is defined in terms of "identity" (to say that p_2 is the only person at t_2 bearing R to p_1 is to say that (x) (if x bears R at t_2 to p_1, then $x = p_2$). Our account of identity, however, rules out the possibility of this problem in a non-ad hoc fashion. It is easy to see why it does. Let us suppose that the relation R in question is the relation of having all of one's properties in common. Could both p_2 and p_3 (where $p_2 \neq p_3$) bear that relation to p_1? For that to take place, p_1 would have to be identical with p_2 (since p_2 certainly has the property of-being-identical-with-p_2) and with p_3 (since p_3 certainly has the property of-being-identical-with-p_3). But then p_2 would be identical with p_3, and, ex hypothesi, they are not. So p_2 and p_3 cannot both bear the relation of having all of their properties in common to p_1, and the splitting problem cannot arise on our account.

What would we say, however, if a splitting case seemed to occur, if we had a p_2 and a p_3 whose memories and/or bodies were continuous with p_1? Our answer to that question is straightforward enough: what we will say depends upon which answer gives rise to the best description and explanation of what has occurred. We may say that p_1 went out of existence and p_2 and p_3 came into existence, we may identify p_1 with one but not the other, or we may go back and challenge the nonidentity of p_2 and p_3. We cannot now say philosophically what would be the best account.

Once more, the difference between our approach and the approach of Parfit, Perry, and Prior is about the nature of the crisis posed by splitting cases. They see the very possibility of such a case as posing a conceptual crisis about identity. I say that only the actual occurrence of such cases would pose a crisis, and it would be a scientific crisis about how to describe and explain what has occurred. It seems to me that this result of my theory of identity is another reason for preferring it to the more classical theories of personal identity or their modifications by such writers as Parfit, Perry, and Prior. After all, since such cases do not occur, and it is only their occurrence that would cause a problem on my account, it follows that there is, at the moment, no splitting problem if my account is true.

3.3 PROBLEMATIC ENTITIES

Our theory of identity has been put forward as a general theory of identity, and it should, therefore, be applicable to all entities. Moreover, it should insure that there are no entities the conditions for whose identity are questionable. Many philosophers have felt, however, that there are such entities, either concrete (such as events or actions) or abstract (such as properties). Some have even concluded that some of them (the abstract ones) do not, therefore, really exist. We shall consider, in this section, the implications of our general theory of identity for these entities. This consideration should also serve to strengthen the case for our account of identity, as it will show its ability to deal with problems of identity that otherwise seem highly problematic.

3.3a Properties and Sets

It is often claimed that there is an important difference between the identity-conditions for sets and properties. Thus, Quine says: "we shall find that those further purposes of attributes are well served by classes, which, after all, are like attributes except for their identity conditions. Classes raise no perplexities over identity, being identical if and only if their members are identical."[17] And some philosophers, most notably Quine, have taken this difference as a reason for renouncing any ontological commitment to properties. Given that the identity-conditions for properties are unclear, Quine argues, we should make do with other abstract entities such as sets, open sentences, and general terms.

From the point of view of our theory, this whole discussion is wrong. The conditions for the identity of properties A and B are not different from the conditions for the identity of sets a and b. They are identical if they have all of their properties in common. From the point of view of the theory of identity, there is no reason for preferring to be committed to one type of entity rather than another.

There are, however, two crucial points to be noted here:

First, saying that the identity conditions for the two types of entities are identical is not to say that the difference between these types of entities are illusory. On the contrary, sets are identical if they have the same membership, although properties are not necessarily identical even if they have the same extension. Our theory will not only accommodate this difference; it will explain it (as we shall see below). All that is being claimed is that this difference is not due to a difference in the definition of identity. Second, set theoreticians have often claimed that they have a choice about a number of ways of introducing identity into the theory of sets, that these ways are formally equivalent, and that there is no basis for choosing between them.[18] Our theory will provide such a basis. Let us look at each of these points more carefully.

Let us first see why properties are not necessarily identical even if they have the same extension. The following proof shows that this is so and also why it is so:

(1)   consider properties F and G that have the same extensions but that are such that C is a condition for having F while not a condition for having G.

(2)   Then F has the property of-having-C-as-a-condition-for-applying-to-an-object, while G does not have that property.

(3) $F \neq G$.

Another similar proof is:

(4)   consider properties F and G that have the same extensions but that need not (presumably because there are different conditions for having the properties in question, conditions that are as a matter of fact satisfied by the same objects but that need not be).

(5) F has the property of-necessarily-having-the-same-extension-as-F.

(6) G does not.

(7) $F \neq G$.

The crucial point behind each of these proofs is that, where properties are concerned, having the same extension does not guarantee having all of one's properties in common, and does not, therefore, guarantee identity.

Neither of these proofs could be run for sets. How would the first run? It would presumably run as follows:

(1') consider sets a and b that have the same membership but that are such that condition C is a condition for belonging to a but not for belonging to b.

(2') Then a has the property of-having-C-as-a-condition-for-membership, while b does not.

(3') $a \neq b$.

The trouble with this proof is that it uses in an unacceptable fashion the idea of a condition for membership in a set. Suppose that a is the set $\{\alpha, \beta, \lambda\}$ as is b, and $\{\alpha, \beta, \lambda\}$ is the set of all and only white horses and of all and only the horses I love, and $'a'$ is "the set of white horses" and $'b'$ is "the set of all the horses that I love." Then one might be tempted to run this proof through by saying that being white is a condition for membership in a but not for membership in b. Although tempting, this would be a mistake. If all that is meant by "being a condition for membership in" is "being satisfied by all objects that are in fact members of," then being white is a condition for membership in both. If, however, "being a condition for membership in" means "is satisfied by all objects in all possible worlds in which they are members of," then being white is a condition for membership in neither. In some possible world in which only α and β were white, λ would still be a member of the set a ($\{\alpha, \beta, \lambda\}$) which we, in this world, identify as the class of white horses; so being white is not a condition, in this sense, of membership in the class of white horses.

The point here is rather simple: while having a certain property (such as being white) may be a necessary condition for having another property (being a white horse) in the strong sense that in any possible world in which one has the latter one has the former, it is not the case that having the former property (being white) is a necessary condition for being a member of the set that corresponds to the latter property (the set of white horses) in the strong sense that in any possible world in which one belongs to that set (that set of objects that we pick out in the actual world by calling them the set of white horses) one has the former property.

The second analogous proof is undercut by the same considerations. It would presumably run as follows:

(4')   consider sets a and b that have the same membership but need not.

(5') a has the property of-necessarily-having-the-same-membership-as-a.

(6') b does not.

(7') $a \neq b$.

Proposition (4') is of course in error. Any given set has of necessity the membership that it does. What has happened here is simply a confusion. If "b" is "the class of horses I love," it is true that there might be another world in which "the class of horses I love" refers to a set with a different membership. But this does not mean that the class of horses I love (the class that I am now picking out by use of that expression) might have a different membership.

What we have shown, then, is the following: there are proofs that show that properties are not necessarily identical even if they have the same extensions, but analogous proofs cannot be constructed for sets. These proofs are based upon our theory that the identity-conditions for all these entities are the same. So our theory can account for the differences between properties and classes.

It is important to note that we have not proved that sets are identical when they have the same membership; we have merely blocked proofs that purport to show that they need not be. This leads us to our second point, the status of the axiom of extensionality if our account is correct.

There are a number of ways in which identity can be introduced into set theory viewed as an applied first-order logic (if the underlying logic is a second-order logic, we could just introduce identity by our definition). One can define identity using extentionality as follows:

$$x = y =_{\text{def}}(z) (z\epsilon x \equiv z\epsilon y) \tag{A}$$

Or one can define it as follows:

$$x = y =_{\text{def}}(z) (x\epsilon z \equiv y\epsilon z) \tag{B}$$

Or one can treat it as a notion indefinable in a first-order system, and treat A and B as axioms [if one uses A (B) as a definition, one will of course be treating B (A) as an axiom].

From the point of view of our theory of identity, the most illuminating approach is the last of these. To adopt (A) as a definition would be to fall into the trap of supposing that identity should be defined separately and differently for different types of entities. The same thing has to be said about adopting (B) as a definition. One might suppose that adopting (B) is better; after all, if we suppose that there is, for each property, a set of objects having that property (and vice versa), then (B) comes close to our definition of identity. The trouble with using (B) as a definition, however, is that it works only if those suppositions are true; if they are not, you might have two sets that belong to the same sets but do not have the same properties, and that would make them identical given the purported definition, even though they really are not.

In short, then, it would be best to treat (A) and (B) as axioms. They express additional assumptions about sets, ones that do not follow from the definition of "identity." These assumptions are:

(1) if two sets have all of their properties in common, then they have the same members (this would be provable if we could assume that having a certain membership is a property of a set);

(2) if two sets have all of their members in common, they have all of their properties in common (this is the assumption of extensionality; it would be prov-

able if we could assume that the only properties
had by sets were properties that followed from the
property of having the membership that it does);

(3) if two sets have all of their properties in common,
they belong to the same sets (this would be provable if we could assume that when a set belongs to
another set, it has the property of belonging to that
other set);

(4) if two sets belong to the same sets, they have all of
their properties in common (this would be provable if we could assume that, for any property,
there is a set that an object belongs to only if it has
that property).

As assumptions, we have no objection to these claims. But
they should not be viewed as defining identity for sets.

3.3.b Events and Actions

There has been considerable discussion in recent years
about the conditions for the identity of events a and b. Our
theory leaves little room for this discussion, since it says
that the conditions for the identity of events are the same as
the conditions for the identity of any entities. Nevertheless,
it would be useful to see the implications of our theory for
the claims that have been advanced by the various partici-
pants in the discussion.

Goldman, in the beginning of *A Theory of Human Action*,
contrasts two approaches to the identity of events and actions, the Anscombe-Davidson approach and the Austin-
Kim approach.[19] One way of seeing the difference between
these approaches is to consider a case in which a person flips
a light switch, turns on the light, and illuminates the room.
How many actions has he performed? According to the
former approach, he has performed only one; according to
the latter approach, he has performed three. Let us look at
the implications of our theory for both of these approaches.

What theory of identity lies behind the former approach?
Davidson puts his theory as follows:[20]

$x = y$ just if (z) (z caused $x \equiv z$ caused y), and
(z) (x caused $z \equiv y$ caused z)

Events and actions are identical just in case they have the same causes and effects.

It is easy to see that this account is inadequate as an account of the sufficient conditions for the identity of events. Two events can have the same cause and the same effects and still be two just because they differ in other properties and do not, therefore, even satisfy Leibniz's Law. Two examples of how this could come about are: (i) events b and c are caused by the same a. They are not identical because they have many different properties. Some catastrophe destroys both b and c before they have any effects. Then b and c satisfy Davidson's sufficient condition for identity, but are not really identical; (ii) events a and b are uncaused and have no effects. They are not identical because they have many different properties. Then a and b satisfy Davidson's sufficient condition for identity but are not really identical (Davidson's theory has the unfortunate result that there can be only one event not causally related to other events).

Is having the same causes and effects at least necessary for the identity of events a and b? Our theory says that it is, providing that we can assume that having a certain cause or having certain effects is a property of the event that has that cause or effect. Suppose that a has a cause (an effect) that b does not. Then a would have a property (the property of having that cause [effect]) that b does not have, and they could not be identical.

But is this assumption sound? At least some philosophers have argued that it is not. They claim that the causal context (———is the cause of ———) is nonextensional, and it is so just because having a certain cause or having a certain effect is not a property of the event that has that cause or effect. Monroe Beardsley has recently presented this case forcefully.[21] Beardsley argues, for example, that

(1)   the piece of wood is burning = the piece of wood is burning yellow

(2)   the presence of sodium in the wood is the cause of its burning yellow

(3)   the presence of sodium in the wood is not the cause of its burning

are a consistent triad, just because the causal content is not extensional.

Again, he argues,

(4)   Socrates's dying = Xantippes's being widowed

(5)   Socrates's drinking hemlock caused Socrates's dying

(6)   Socrates's drinking hemlock did not cause Xantippes's being widowed

are a consistent triad, made consistent because the causal context is not extensional.

I am not very persuaded by this argument, primarily because I do not see that the triads are consistent. I suspect that Beardsley thinks that we must find the triads consistent, because all the claims in them are (in certain situations) jointly true, but this too seems in error. I suspect that in the envisaged situations, claims (2) and (6) are false. Let us look first at (2). No doubt, the presence of sodium in the wood plays a major role in the explanation of the yellowness in the burning, but it would be wrong to infer from that that the presence is the cause of that event which is both the burning of the wood and the yellow burning of the wood. To make this inference is to confuse causes with explanations. Again, although the fact that Socrates drank hemlock needs to be supplemented by the fact that he was married to Xantippe to explain her being widowed, one cannot infer that Socrates's drinking hemlock did not cause that one event which is both his dying and her being a widow. To make this inference is, once more, to confuse explanations with causes. The point here is, then, simple. Faced with triads like (1) to (3) and (4) to (6), some philosophers would drop (1) and (4), while others, like Beardsley, would accept all the claims and deny the extensionality of causal contexts. I would suggest, as an alternative, dropping claims like (2) and (6) by recognizing that their plausibility derives from a confusion between explanations and causal relations.

Where, then, do we stand? Davidson's necessary condition of same cause and same effects is, we have suggested, probably valid. But his claim that the same condition is sufficient for the identity of events is certainly wrong.

We turn, then, to the implications of our definition of "identity" for the Austin-Kim theory of the identity of events. On that account, as explained by Kim, an event consists of an n-tuple of objects satisfying a given n-adic property at a given time.[22] Roughly speaking, events are identical just in case the objects, time, and property are identical (this needs modifying to allow us to identify such events as Joe's hitting Frank and Frank's being hit by Joe).

Kim's condition is clearly a necessary condition (given our theory or even just given Leibniz's Law) provided that we can assume that among the properties of a given event are that it occurs at a given time t_n and that it involves objects $a \ldots m$ and property p_m. But is his condition sufficient? From the perspective of our theory, that question is whether the satisfaction of his condition insures that the events in question have all of their properties in common.

It is easy to show that the Kim condition, as it stands, is not sufficient (at least given his construal of an event). Imagine a situation in which, at t_1, Roger fires two guns, one in his right hand and one in his left hand, and consider the following events:

E_1 Roger's right-handed firing of a gun at t_1

E_2 Roger's left-handed firing of a gun at t_1

E_3 Roger's firing of a gun at t_1 (this is the event associated with, but maybe not identical with, E_1)

E_4 Roger's firing of a gun at t_1 (this is the event associated with, but maybe not identical with, E_2)

E_3 and E_4 cannot be identical, since one took place in Roger's right hand, while the other took place in Roger's left hand. And yet they both consist of the same person (Roger) having

the same property (being a gun-firer) at the same time (t_1).
The Austin-Kim theory, because it only considered some of
the properties of the event, is clearly not correct.

One cannot, it should be noted, fix things up by construing
an event as an n-tuple of objects satisfying an n-adic property at a given time *in a given place,* and by saying that it is
sufficient, for the identity of *a* and *b,* that they consist of the
same object(s) satisfying the same property at the same time
and place. After all, Davidson has shown that there can be
two different events involving the same object in the same
place and time, and that is sufficient to generate a counterexample to this revised proposal. Using his example of
the top which is both spinning and rotating, we consider the
following events:

E_1' the top's spinning in place at t_1
E_2' the top's heating up at t_1
E_3' the top's undergoing a rotation or heating at t_1 (this
is the event associated with, but maybe not identical with, E_1')
E_4' the top's undergoing a rotation or heating at t_1 (this
is the event associated with, but maybe not identical with, E_2')

E_3' and E_4' cannot be identical, since one is a spinning and the
other is a heating, and yet they both involve the same object
having the same property at the same time in the same
place.

An interesting side point emerges from these examples. It
has often been said that Davidson's theory identifies events
that Kim's theory treats as different, and this is confirmed
by the fact that Davidson, unlike Kim, would identify E_1 and
E_3. But Kim would identify E_3 and E_4, while Davidson would
presumably not, so this oft-repeated remark is not entirely
correct.

The moral of our examination of both Davidson and Kim
is very simple: they would identify events that have certain
properties in common, and this is inadequate because having those properties in common is not sufficient to insure

that the events will have all of their properties in common. It is best, therefore, simply to adopt our general theory of identity and apply it to the identity of events.

The adoption of our theory leads to very desirable results. Many have wanted to find a theory that agrees with Davidson's view that adverbial modification doesn't introduce a new event (that Roger's firing the gun, e_1, is identical with Roger's slowly firing the gun, e_2) while agreeing with Kim's view that this event is not identical with other associated events like Roger's killing the stranger, e_3. I believe that our theory provides just that desirable result.

It is easy to show why, on our theory, Roger's pulling the trigger is not identical with his killing the stranger. A number of familiar arguments show that these two events do not have all of their properties in common. The killing has the property, for example, of being accomplished by means of pulling the trigger, while the pulling of the trigger does not. And the pulling of the trigger is surely a shorter event than the killing. It is harder to show, of course, that e_1 and e_2 are identical, but the following identity of properties suggests that they do have all of their properties in common: (a) the two events involve the same gun, which was fired slowly, and they take place at the same spatiotemporal locations; (b) they have the same causes and effects, although the slowness of the firing will be mentioned in only some explanations; (c) they are performed by the same means. So the claim that these events are identical, given our theory, while not demonstrable, is clearly very plausible.

This result about the identity of events is not new. Writers such as Thomson and Beardsley have advocated it.[23] But they get it only by strong assumptions. Beardsley, for ex-·ample, winds up with this result only by making strong assumptions about the distinction between basic event-properties and dependent event-properties. It is one final merit of our general theory of identity that this desirable result follows directly from it.

FOUR ✦ THE THEORY OF CHANGE

The theory of identity that we have presented and defended in the first part of this book is extremely powerful. In this second part of the book, we shall argue that it is nevertheless incomplete, and that its incompleteness follows from its failure to take into account the implications of an important Aristotelean distinction.

This chapter will begin with a presentation and defense of this Aristotelean distinction. It will then explain why the acceptance of this distinction leads to the recognition that our theory of identity is incomplete. It will also be shown that the acceptance of this distinction gives rise to a very Aristotelean theory of essentialism. These two implications are explored at greater length in the next two chapters.

4.1 THE ARISTOTELEAN DISTINCTION

Aristotle drew an important distinction between two types of changes: alterations, on the one hand, and coming-to-bes and passing-aways (which we will refer to from now on as substantial changes), on the other hand. He set out that distinction as follows:

> Since, then, we must distinguish (a) the substratum, and (b) the property whose nature it is to be predicated of the substratum; and since change of each of these occurs; there is alteration when the substratum is perceptible and persists, but changed in its own properties, the properties in question being opposed to one another either as contraries or as intermediaries. . . . But when nothing perceptible persists in its identity as a substratum, and the thing changes as a whole . . . such an

occurrence is no longer alteration. It is a coming-to-be of the one substance and a passing-away of the other. . . . If, however, in such cases, any property persists in the thing that has come-to-be the same way as it was in the thing which has passed-away, . . . the second thing, into which the first changes, must not be a property of this persistent identical something. Otherwise, the change will be alteration.[1]

In other words, if, before the change, there was an object o_1 that had a property P_1, then the change is an alteration if o_1 continues to exist after the change but now has a property P_2 whose possession is incompatible with the possession of P_1, while the change is a substantial change if, after its occurrence, o_1 no longer exists even if there is some o_2 ($\neq o_1$) which has P_1.

There are several points to be noted about this distinction: to begin with, this theory of substantial change is perfectly compatible with the view that there is something that persists through all changes.[2] Some of the properties of the old object can persist in the new one. More importantly, it is perfectly possible for o_1 and o_2 to be composed out of the same thing or things. They could, for example, be composed out of the same particles of matter. All that is necessary is that these permanent entities are not the only subjects of predication, that o_1 and o_2 also be subjects of predication. This is an extremely important point. After all, there is a very attractive view that a goal of science is to discover some underlying permanencies that persist through all changes. Some have suggested that the discovery of these permanencies will show that nothing ever stops existing or begins existing, that all that happens is that these permanencies are altered. This suggestion is mistaken. As we have just seen, the Aristotelean distinction is not challenged by any such discoveries. It is interesting that Aristotle seems to have been aware of this point. For his own reasons, he had adopted the very strong claim that there must be something that persists through any change, something other than ordinary substances that do not persist through substantial change. This is why he postulated the existence of matter: "Matter, in the most proper sense of the term, is to be identified with the substratum of coming-to-be and passing-away."[3] But he saw that, despite all of this, he could maintain the distinction between substantial change and alteration.

A second point to note is the following: it is sometimes supposed that it is a matter of convention whether or not a given change is an alteration or a substantial change, that is, that it is a matter of convention whether a given o_1 persists through a given change; this seems to be a mistake. Is it, for example, a matter of convention whether we continue to exist after our death? And if so, why haven't we insured our immortality a long time ago? More seriously, it seems obviously true that trees stop existing when they are burned down, but not when they lose a branch, and that this was true a long time before there were people who had conventions about the identity of trees. So our distinction cannot be based upon conventions. To be sure, there are undoubtedly many cases in which we have to decide whether what has occurred is an alteration or a substantial change, and this has perhaps led some people to suppose that the whole distinction is merely a matter of convention. That is, however, a weak argument; it could, after all, be applied equally to all distinctions about which there are borderline cases, viz. to all distinctions. The existence of decisions merely indicates that there are borderline cases, not that the distinction is based upon convention.

It has been suggested that there is another basis for the claim that Aristotle's distinction rests upon convention.[4] The idea is this: our experience comes to us without being divided up into objects. It is we who, as a matter of convention, apply to that undifferentiated experience a certain conceptual scheme, one that involves such things as trees. We could, using a different convention, divide up our experience so that it contained no trees, and hence no trees that undergo substantial change when they burn. In this way, it might be argued, it is a matter of convention that a certain substantial change has occurred.

This line of argument raises many questions that cannot be discussed here. These include the questions as to whether our experience is undifferentiated in the relevant way, and whether it is true that it is a matter of convention that we differentiate objects in the way that we do. But there is one point that we must note here, one that is, I believe, sufficient to undercut the appeal of this line of argument. One must distinguish the following two claims:

(a) it is a matter of convention that we distinguish out of our undifferentiated experience certain experiences that we describe as experiences of a tree;

(b) it is a matter of convention that there actually is a tree that, among other things, we are experiencing at a given time.

Whatever the plausibility of (a), (b) seems extremely unlikely. In order for it to be true, it would have to be the case that there were no trees until the convention of distinguishing trees was adopted, and that seems just wrong. And if only (a) is plausible, this whole line of argument becomes irrelevant to the issue before us. That there are trees and that they go out of existence when they burn down, and that all of this is nonconventional, is perfectly compatible with the truth of (a). I conclude, therefore, that this whole line of argument is irrelevant to our issue, and that we have no reason to deny the nonconventionality of the truth that certain changes are substantial changes, while other changes are mere alterations.

Much as it is sometimes supposed (incorrectly, as we have seen) that the Aristotelean distinction is merely conventional, so it is sometimes supposed that whether a given change is an alteration or a substantial change depends upon how we classify the objects involved when we refer to them. Thus it is sometimes supposed that whether a change in color of my desk constitutes a substantial change depends upon whether I refer to it by use of "my red desk" or by use of "my desk." If I use the former, a change in color must be a substantial change (after all, my red desk must remain red). If I use the latter, a change in color needn't be a substantial change (after all, my desk need not be red). This supposition is also in error. The distinction antedates any language, so it cannot be language-dependent. Moreover, there is nothing incoherent with the claim "my red desk will be painted green tomorrow," so the claim seems straightforwardly false. Even if I refer to my desk as "my red desk," taking advantage of the fact that the desk is at the moment red, that in no way imparts any special status to the desk's being red.

Two final points should be noted about this distinction: first, it is applicable to changes involving both concrete and abstract objects. In the case of abstract objects, however, something very strange happens. While one can imagine alterations involving abstract objects—four was once my favorite number but it isn't any more—it seems impossible for there to be a substantial change involving one. This is due to the fact—at least, to what we all assume is a fact, for reasons that are unclear—that abstract objects exist necessarily and cannot go out of existence as they would if they were involved in substantial changes.

Second, this distinction is one that we are all quite familiar with and can use, quite comfortably, in many cases in which questions of identity and continued existence are of importance. One notable example of its use occurs when we think about human death. What makes us treat it so differently from other changes involving human beings is precisely that it, but not the other changes, is the going-out-of-existence-of, and not merely an alteration in, the person in question. This distinction is also used, of course, in more prosaic cases. If your car is insured, then lots of things can happen to your car and it will still be insured (unless, of course, the insurance is formally canceled). It can be painted, you can change the engine, and so on. But if it is entirely flattened and made into sheet metal, from which a car is then made, your insurance would not cover the new car, since the new car is not identical with your old car. The changes that the old car underwent, unlike the paint job and the engine job, were substantial changes and not mere alterations.

The Aristotelean distinction is then based neither upon conventions nor on our way of classifying objects, is applicable without any difficulty in many cases, and is applicable to both concrete and abstract objects. It is not surprising, therefore, that this distinction is widely accepted in philosophy. But as it has been ingeniously challenged by Majorie Price, we should look at it more carefully before we examine its implications.[5]

There are two sorts of examples used by Price, one involving the transformation of objects, and the other involving the dismantling of objects. Let us look at each of them separately. Price first describes a case of a dog Rover that undergoes a transformation that results in another entity, Clover, which is an amorphous mass of cells whose chromosomal constitution has changed. She then argues as follows against the claim that a dog's stopping to be a dog is a substantial change (her example of a typical Aristotelean claim):

> No one can deny that the entity in the isolation unit at the end of the interval in question, call it "Clover," is Rover, the object confined there six months earlier. That is, one cannot claim that Rover ceased to exist at some time during that period. For no organism died: the cells composing the spatio-temporally continuous Rover and Clover never ceased functioning. Yet we cannot justifiably classify Clover as a dog. For the only biologically significant property Clover shares with any dog that ever lived is the property of being composed of cells. . . . Consequently, one can and must describe the Rover-Clover case as one in which something was a dog (terrier) at one moment in its existence and not a dog (terrier) at another moment of its existence.[6]

The rest of her argument is devoted to arguing (a) that this is not a case of identity through metamorphosis; and (b) that the identity of Rover and Clover conforms, as it must, to Leibniz's Law.

I would like to focus in on her initial argument that Rover = Clover. The crux of her argument is simply this: "no organism died: the cells composing the spatio-temporally continuous Rover and Clover never ceased functioning." As an argument, this is very unconvincing. To be sure, organisms as we know them go out of existence by dying, and when an organism has not died, it has not gone out of existence. This is true, however, only because organisms do not undergo the type of transformation that Price is envisaging (except for the admittedly different case of metamorphosis). If organisms did, I would see no reason to continue to accept the view that organisms continue to exist until they die. In light of the circumstances envisaged, especially those involving the radical differences between Rover and Clover, I submit that we do best in such circumstances to treat them as nonidentical and to recognize that organisms can go out of existence without dying.

There is, of course, one difficulty here. In the case envisaged by Price, the transformation from Rover to Clover is continuous, and there is no sharp dividing point. So there will be an ambiguous period during which it is unclear whether we have here Rover or Clover. But that will of course also be a period in which it is ambiguous whether or not we have here a dog. And the crucial point is that there will clearly be no period in which Rover still exists but not as a dog.

One final remark: it is useful to compare Price's case with the case of Gregor envisaged by Kafka in his *Metamorphosis*. Gregor's case is also not like the standard cases of biological metamorphosis. And yet we are inclined to identify Gregor in the morning with Gregor of the night before. We are also, however, inclined to treat him as a human being in the body of a bug. This is because of the many similarities of personality and memory that remain through the transformation. There are enough to allow Gregor in the morning still to be a human being as he was the night before, and still to be Gregor. But in Price's case, the change is complete, and there is no reason to treat Clover as a dog. I submit, however, that there is also no reason to treat Clover as identical with Rover, and this type of transformation poses no problem for the Aristotelean distinction.

Price's second type of case involves the disassembly of objects. What she is looking for is an object of a type F that exists at t_1 (where F is a type such that, if we adopt the Aristotelean distinction, we would normally think that the loss of F means the going-out-of-existence of the object), is disassembled between t_1 and t_2 and is, therefore, no longer an F, and is reassembled and exists again as an F at t_2. Given such an object, she would conclude that the Aristotelean distinction is wrong, for the object is no longer an F between t_1 and t_2 and yet still exists. Finding even an example is, she admits, not very easy. Consider a watch that is disassembled and then reassembled. We would certainly identify the watch through the whole process, but, Price concedes, we would also think of it as a disassembled watch during its period of disassembly. So, as a watch through the whole period, it could not be used as a counterexample. Price's example involves this case in which "F" stands for "is an organism":

Using microsurgical techniques, Smith, a Rockworth University scientist, at time t_1 dissects John, a well scrutinized E. *coli* bacterium. . . . After isolating John's two chromosomes and its ribosomes, Smith transfers to a test tube the aqueous solution he drained from John's interior by means of a micro pipette and stores the remaining cell membrane and wall in separate test tubes. Several days later, having ascertained that none of the cell parts are functioning, Smith reassembles them. An injection of substance XYZ at time t_2 animates the reassembled cell . . . it exhibits all the vital properties had by living E. *coli* bacteria. It seems to me that one can and must describe this as a case in which something ceased to be an organism without ceasing to exist: John ceased to be an organism at t_1, continued to exist as a scattered material object between t_1 and t_2, and became an organism again at t_2.[7]

This type of example raises two very difficult questions: (a) is there any reason to believe that John exists during the period of disassembly? and (b) is there any reason to believe that John, if he exists, is not an organism during that period? Price must, of course, show that the answer to both of these questions is yes, but I do not see that she succeeds.

She carefully considers the view that John goes out of existence, is replaced by the sum of John's dissociated parts, which is in turn superseded by a new bacterium composed out of John's components. She argues against that view as follows:

> The experiment I imagined returns the parts of the disassembled object to the state they were in before Smith dissociated them. . . . This dissimilarity is clearly of consequence for the question whether the subject of the change remains the same. For proof of this, consider . . . were the pieces of a fragmented jug (or a smashed table) rejoined to make an object of the same design and size as the one that broke. . . . We would instead say that the jug (table) that results from rejoining the pieces is the very same thing as the jug (table) that broke.[8]

This argument seems to be a nonsequitur. To be sure, there are very good reasons for identifying the reassembled table with the original table, and there are equally good reasons for identifying the reassembled organism with John. But is there any reason for supposing that the object in question existed during the period of disassociation? Isn't it equally reasonable to suppose that it has gone out of existence when disassembled and come back into existence when reassembled? If it isn't, I cannot see that Price has given us the slightest reason for supposing so.

This possibility of interrupted existence has not been sufficiently considered in the literature, so let me say a little more about it. Given our theory of identity, it is relatively easy to give meaning to this possibility. What is envisaged is an object a that exists until t_1, an object b that exists from some later time t_2 to a still later time, and a community of properties, among a and b, at any given moment of time. It is hard to see what is wrong with this idea. Locke, to be sure, argued against it on the grounds that no object can have two beginnings of existence,[9] and this argument has been endorsed by such subtle thinkers as Reid.[10] It is, however, a bad argument. If by "beginning of existence" one means "first moment of existence," then an object with interrupted existence has only one beginning. If, however, one means "first moment of existence after a period of nonexistence," then objects with interrupted existence have two beginnings of existence, but there is nothing incoherent with that.

I have not been arguing that John's existence is an example of interrupted existence. I think that that is a plausible claim, but there is the other plausible possibility (to be discussed in a moment) that John's existence is continuous and he continuously exists as an organism. All that I want to conclude at this point is that Price has offered no argument at all for the claim that John exists during the period of disassembly. She only thinks that she has, because she has confused that question with the very different question about whether the reassembled entity is identical with John.

We turn then to the second question raised by the case of John, whether there is any reason to suppose that John, if he exists while disassembled, is not an organism. It is very hard to make out Price's argument at this point; she concedes (hesitantly) that disassembled watches are watches, but fervently denies that disassembled stereos are stereos and disassembled organisms are organisms. I cannot see her basis for this distinction, and some of her intuitions seem to me to be downright odd (I see nothing odd about pointing to my temporarily disassembled stereo components and referring to them as my stereo set). The question as to when a disassembled F is an F is a difficult one; it seems to be connected to such diverse factors as the intentions of those who disassembled it and of those who might reassemble it, the probability and/or difficulty of reassembling, the uniqueness and/or value of the object, and so on. And most crucially, these factors are also relevant to determining whether the object which used to be an F still exists in a disassembled fashion. So without deciding about the case of John (we don't really have the context needed to decide), it would seem best to conclude that if John does exist in the disassembled period (as opposed to later on, when reassembled), he is also an organism during that period.

I think then that we can draw the following conclusions: Price has by no means established that there exist any counterexamples to the Aristotelean thesis of change. Moreover, but perhaps more tentatively, the best ways of analyzing her examples seem to be perfectly compatible with the ordinary Aristotelean theory of change. We will, therefore, continue to work with that distinction, and look at its implications in the next section.

4.2 Its Implications

Aristotle distinguished the essential from the accidental properties of an object. The rough idea that he seemed to have in mind was that an object's essential properties were possessed by the object necessarily, and were constitutive of the nature of the object. Recent philosophers have not always accepted the legitimacy of this Aristotelean distinction. But, as we shall see briefly now and more fully in the next chapter, one implication of Aristotle's distinction among changes is that the distinction between essential and accidental properties is legitimate. This is so because the essentialist distinction can be drawn on the basis of the distinction among changes.

We shall say that an object o_1 has a property P_1 essentially just in case o_1 has P_1 and would go out of existence if it lost it, just in case the loss of it would involve a substantial change. We shall say that an object o_1 has a property P_1 accidentally just in case o_1 has P_1 but could lose it without going out of existence, that is, just in case the loss of it would involve a mere alteration.

In light of what we have seen so far about the distinction between changes, the following seems to follow about the essentialist distinction: it is based neither upon conventions nor on our way of classifying objects, it is applicable without any difficulty in many cases, and it is applicable to both concrete and abstract objects.

We shall return to a discussion, elaboration, and modification of this theory of essentialism in the next chapter, where we will also compare it to some of the recently discussed alternatives. For now we merely want to suggest that one implication of the distinction between changes is that there is also a distinction between essential and accidental properties.

The distinction between essential and accidental properties that we have just briefly sketched is a distinction among the properties of existing objects. It says nothing about possible but nonactual objects and their properties. It is interesting to consider the question of whether it could be extended to merely possible objects. However, that raises so many preliminary questions about their status and about the properties that they possess that it seems better to consider these issues in a separate study.

The second implication of Aristotle's distinction among changes is that the theory of identity presented in the first part of this book is incomplete. In order to see why, one must look at the implications of the notion of substantial change for identity through time. Consider some object o_1 of a type T which exists at t_1, where T and o_1 are such that o_1's losing T means o_1's going out of existence. Consider further some object o_2 at t_2 which lacks T. According to Aristotle's theory of change, o_1 cannot be identical with o_2, since its being identical with o_2 would mean its continuing to exist from t_1 to t_2 even while losing T. On our original theory, however, there was no reason why o_1 could not be identical with o_2. All that was required was that they both have the same properties (including T) at t_1 and the same properties (including $\bar{T}$) at t_2. So the addition of these Aristotelean notions about change modifies our theory of identity through time.

It is not surprising that this has happened. What the theory of change introduces is a new set of necessary conditions for an object o_2 at t_2 being identical with an object o_1 at an earlier t_1. These necessary conditions are that o_2 must have retained some of its properties that it had at t_1, the ones that o_1 cannot lose without going out of existence.

All of this is extremely problematic. On the one hand, can't we borrow our own arguments from Chapter Three (where we argued against a variety of additional necessary conditions) to show that these additional conditions are not necessary? On the other hand, how can we deny the legitimacy of these conditions in light of the fact that they follow from the Aristotelean theory of change? These are the questions that we shall have to consider in Chapter Six.

FIVE ◆ THE THEORY OF ESSENTIALISM

5.1 THE NATURE OF A THEORY OF ESSENTIALISM AND ITS PROBLEMS

In 4.2, we saw in a very preliminary fashion that our Aristotelean theory of change gives rise to a distinction between the essential and accidental properties of an object. We shall, in this chapter, look at the generated distinction more carefully. Before doing so, however, it may be helpful if we were to say something in a preliminary way about the intuitive idea behind the distinction, and the problems it faces.

What is the basic idea behind the claim that there is a distinction between the properties that an object has essentially and the properties that an object has accidentally? It seems to be the following: on the one hand, there are some properties that an object must have; if the object didn't have them, it wouldn't exist at all. These are the properties that an object has essentially. On the other hand, there are some properties that an object has but that it might not have. The possession of these properties is not necessary for the object's existence. These are the properties that an object has accidentally.

Two obvious questions are raised by this distinction: (a) what does it mean to say that an object must have a property, as opposed to merely saying that it has the property? (b) how can we tell which properties are had by an object essentially and which are had by an object accidentally? It is important to keep in mind that these are two different (although obviously related) questions. One concerns itself with the meaning of certain claims, while the other concerns itself with how we come to know whether these claims are true or false. And it might be the case (although I think that it is not) that we know what these claims mean without knowing how to tell whether they are true or false.

All of the theories of essentialism that we will be considering, including the one suggested in 4.2, attempt to answer or avoid these questions. In addition, however, they must also be able to answer or avoid certain objections to essentialism that have been raised in recent years. What are these objections? There are three of them, one having to do with referential opacity, one having to do with the different classes to which objects belong, and one having to do with the problem of identity through possible worlds.[1] Since the first two are now known to be in error, I will just briefly explain what they are and what is wrong with them,[2] and focus in on the third problem, the problem that any theory of essentialism must handle and that relates in important ways to our question (a).

As far as referential opacity is concerned, the objection runs as follows: consider the claim that

(1)   nine is essentially greater than seven

and

(2)   the number that I am thinking about now is essentially greater than seven,

and suppose that I am now thinking about nine. Then, these claims should both be true or both be false, since they both say of the same object that it has the same property essentially. But, so the argument goes, (1) is true and (2) is false. After all, I could have been thinking about five and then the number that I would be thinking about now would be less than seven. So there is something wrong with essentialist claims, and they should be rejected. The answer to this objection is very simple: (2) is true, just as (1) is, for the number that I am thinking about now could not be altered so as to be less than seven. I could be altered, of course, to think about a number less than seven, but that is irrelevant to the truth of (2). Or, in other words, the reason why one thinks that (2) is false is that I could have been thinking about some other number which is less than seven, but all that that shows is that the very different claim that

(2') "the number that I am thinking about now is greater than seven" is necessarily true

is false. As long as you do not reinterpret (2) so that it means (2'), and no essentialist should reinterpret his essentialist claims in this fashion, there is no problem with referential opacity.

A similar error is committed by the objection from the fact that objects belong to different classes. It runs as follows: consider, as an example, the claims that

(3)   all cyclists are essentially two-legged but not essentially rational

and that

(4)   all mathematicians are essentially rational but not essentially two-legged,

and consider Joe, who is both a mathematician and two-legged. It seems to follow from the truth of the above claims that Joe both is and is not essentially two-legged and essentially rational. So our essentialist claims have led us to a contradiction and essentialism should therefore be rejected. The answer to this objection is once more very simple: both (3) and (4) are false since cyclists are not essentially two-legged (a cyclist can lose a leg and still continue to exist, although he cannot cycle anymore) and mathematicians are not essentially rational (a mathematician can stop being rational and still continue to exist, although he cannot then do any more mathematics). The only reason why one might think that (3) and (4) are true is because one is confusing them with the true claims that

(3')   "all cyclists are two-legged" is necessarily true while "all cyclists are rational" is not

and that

(4′) "all mathematicians are rational" is necessarily true while "all mathematicians are two-legged" is not.

So long as one does not reinterpret (3) and (4) so as to mean (3′) and (4′), and no essentialist should interpret essentialist claims in this fashion, there is no problem about objects like Joe who belong to more than one class. Nothing, after all, follows from claims like (3′) and (4′) about which properties are had essentially by whom.

We come then to the much more serious problem of identity through possible worlds. What has essentialism to do with identity through possible worlds, and why is there a problem about identity through possible worlds? To deal with the first question first, the believer in essentialism believes that objects have properties necessarily. We have already asked what this means, and one standard answer is that it means that there are properties that are not merely had by an object in the actual world, but which would be had by it in all possible worlds (or, at least, all in which it exists). And this seems equivalent to the idea that the property in question is had by it in the actual world and by the object identical to it in any given possible world (or, at least, in any world in which there is an object identical to it). So, it would appear, essentialist claims are equivalent to claims involving the concept of identity through possible worlds, and are therefore meaningful only if that notion is meaningful. As far as the second question is concerned, it is easy to see that the notion of identity through possible worlds cannot be the same as the ordinary notion of identity. Consider, for example, two actual physical objects o_1 and o_2. We have argued that they are identical just in case they have all of their properties in common at all instances of time. But this cannot be so if o_1 is an actual object and o_2 exists in some possible world. After all, it seems as though an object could be, in a possible world, in some very different place than it is in in the actual world, so we have to allow for the possibility that o_1 is identical with o_2, even though o_1 is in p_1 at t_1 while

o_2 is in a very different place p_2 at t_1 and does not therefore have all of its properties in common with o_1. The identity of an actual object with a possible object does not therefore involve any requirement of having all properties in common, so we must be employing a different conception of identity when we talk about their identity.

It is often thought that the problem of identity through possible worlds is a problem about how we can tell, of some object in a possible world, which, if any, object in the actual world it is identical with, that is, that the problem of identity through possible worlds is an epistemological problem. That is not the real problem. After all, even if one could not tell in many (or even all) cases, it would not follow, unless one was using some very suspicious verificationist assumption, that there is something wrong with the concept of identity through possible worlds. Remember our distinction above between questions (1) and (2). The real problem is that it is unclear as to what it means for an actual entity e_1 to be identical with an entity e_2 that exists in a possible world, and it is therefore unclear as to what any claim, such as an essentialist claim, that involves this concept of identity through possible worlds, means.

Our result is consonant with Kit Fine's argument to show that a sentence has a de dicto equivalent iff its truth does not turn upon identity through possible worlds. As Fine himself says, "this result, then, substantiates the common philosophical view that one who would make essential use of quantifying in must also make sense of cross-world identity."[3]

This failure to distinguish between the epistemological problem of trans-world identity and the problem of its very meaning, and to recognize that the crucial problem is the second one, is particularly noticeable in Alvin Plantinga's *The Nature of Necessity*. Plantinga begins his discussion by setting out what he takes to be the problem as follows:

But then we must ask ourselves how we could possibly identify Socrates in that world. How could we pick him out? How could we locate him there? How could we possibly tell which of the many things contained in W is Socrates? If we try to employ the properties we use to identify him in this world, our efforts may well end in dismal failure. . . . But if we cannot identify him in W, so the argument continues, then we do not really understand the assertion that he exists there. If we cannot even identify him, we would not know whom we are talking about, in saying that Socrates exists in that world or has this or that property therein.[4]

Plantinga rightly rejects that argument as a sophism:

A possible world is a possible state of affairs. In saying that an individual x exists or has a property P in a state of affairs S, we are pointing to the impossibility that S obtains and x fails to exist or fails to have P. So, for example, consider the state of affairs consisting in Socrates' being a carpenter, and call this state of affairs "S." Does Socrates exist in S? Obviously: had this state of affairs been actual, he would have existed. But is there a problem of identifying him, picking him out, in S—that is, must we look into S to see which thing therein in Socrates? Must there be or must we know of some empirically manifest property he had in this and every other state of affairs in which he exists? Surely not.[5]

What Plantinga does not realize is that none of this speaks to the real problem of identity across possible worlds. The real question, in understanding the claim that Socrates might have been a carpenter in terms of a possible world in which there is something identical with Socrates which is a carpenter, is whether we can make sense of the claim that the object in question is identical with Socrates. Plantinga's correct epistemological point that we needn't (and in fact can't) pick the object out is irrelevant to this crucial question. Contrary to what is often thought, then, Plantinga has not shown that there is no problem of cross-world identity.

5.2 Kaplan and Plantinga

There are two theories of essentialism that have appeared recently and have attracted much attention. These are the theories of David Kaplan and Alvin Plantinga.[6] I should like, in this section, to explain these theories; in the next section, we shall see whether they help us with our problems and whether they face other shortcomings.

The best way to understand the technical aspects of these theories is to begin with the important distinction, drawn by Quine and employed by us in the last section, between claims of the form

(1) necessarily, there is an x that is a P

and claims of the form

(2) there is an x that is necessarily a P.

A similar distinction exists between claims of the form

(3) necessarily, a is a P

and claims of the form

(4) a is necessarily a P.

One of the significant differences between these claims is that claims of the (1) and (3) form, unlike claims of the (2) and (4) form, have a simple and obvious interpretation that is relatively unproblematic. Any claim of the (1) form can be interpreted as a claim of the form

(1′) ⌜there is an x that is a P⌝ is necessarily true

or of the form

(1″) ⌜there is an x that is a P⌝ necessarily expresses a true proposition

or of the form

(1‴) ⌜there is an x that is a P⌝ necessarily expresses a true statement.

Which of these three we choose depends, of course, upon our views as to what is the bearer of truth-values. Similarly, depending upon our views on that topic, we can interpret any claim of form (3) as being of the form

(3′)   ⌜a is a P⌝ is necessarily true

or of the form

(3″)   ⌜a is a P⌝ necessarily expresses a true proposition

or of the form

(3‴)   ⌜a is a P⌝ necessarily expresses a true statement.

(We shall allow truths to be necessary truths provided that they cannot be false; this will enable us to avoid problems of failure of reference in some possible world. Plantinga, as shall see below, has another way of dealing with this problem.) These interpretations, because they entail that the necessity in question is a necessity of a sentence (either a necessity of being true or a necessity of expressing a truth), are known as de dicto interpretations of modal claims.

The situation is very different when we consider claims of the (2) and (4) form. These claims seem to be attributing a necessity to an object, viz. the necessity of possessing a certain property. It is these claims, of course, that are essentialist claims, and that face all of the problems we discussed in the last section.

The simplest way to reinterpret (2) and (4) claims with a de dicto interpretation would be to make them equivalent to the corresponding (1) and (3) claims. Thus, adopting (1′) and (3′) as our interpretation of (1) and (3)—and using corner quotes for uniformity even when simple quotes would do—we would interpret

(5)   nine is necessarily greater than seven

as

(5*)   ⌜nine is greater than seven⌝ is necessarily true

and

(6)   there is some number which is necessarily greater than seven

as

(6*) ⌜there is some number which is greater than seven⌝ is necessarily true.

This simple move will not do. After all, if the number that I am thinking about now is nine, then it will be true (as we saw in the previous section) that

(7) the number that I am now thinking about is necessarily greater than seven

but, according to our reinterpretation, this will be equivalent to

(7*) ⌜the number that I am now thinking about is greater than seven⌝ is necessarily true

and (7*) is false. In other words, this simple de dicto reinterpretation makes too many true claims false.

A second de dicto reinterpretation avoids this difficulty. It makes all claims of the (2) form equivalent to claims of the form

(2**) $(\exists x)\,(\exists \alpha)$ [Denotes (α, x) · ⌜α is a P⌝ is necessarily true]

and all claims of the (4) form equivalent to claims of the form

(4**) $(\exists \alpha)$ [Denotes (α, a) · ⌜α is a P⌝ is necessarily true]

This second de dicto reinterpretation avoids the difficulties that our first reinterpretation faced. After all, it interprets (7) as

(7**) $(\exists \alpha)$ [denotes $(\alpha,$ the number that I am now thinking about) and ⌜α is greater than seven⌝ is necessarily true]

and (7**) is true since "nine" denotes the number that I am now thinking about and "nine is greater than seven" is necessarily true. In other words, unlike the first reinterpretation, the second reinterpretation does not make true modal claims false.

Unfortunately, however, it does make false modal claims true, and must therefore be rejected. After all, if, once more, the number that I am now thinking about is nine, it is false that

>   (8)   nine is necessarily being thought about by me now

But, on this second interpretation, (8) is equivalent to

>   (8**) $(\exists\alpha)$ [Denotes (α, nine) · $\ulcorner\alpha$ is being thought about by me now$\urcorner$ is necessarily true]

and (8**) is true since $\ulcorner$the number which I am thinking about now is being thought about by me now$\urcorner$ is necessarily true. In other words, if the first reinterpretation allows for too few necessary properties of objects, the second reinterpretation allows for too many.

Now, Kaplan would replace (2**) with

> (2^k) $(\exists x)\,(\exists\alpha)$ [Denotes$_{\text{nec.}}$ (α,x) $\ulcorner\alpha$ is a $P\urcorner$ is necessarily true]

and (4**) with

> (4^k) $(\exists\alpha)$ [Denotes$_{\text{nec.}}$ (α,a) · $\ulcorner\alpha$ is a $P\urcorner$ is necessarily true]

in both of these formulas, "Denotes$_{\text{nec.}}$" means that the name denotes the object in question in all possible words. On the other hand, Plantinga would replace (2**) with

> (2^p) $(\exists x)\,(\exists a)\,(Px$ · the proposition expressed by $\ulcorner a$ has non-$P\urcorner$, where "a" is a proper name of that x and "P" is a proper name of P, or the proposition which would be expressed by $\ulcorner a$ has non-$P\urcorner$ if "a" were a proper name of that x and "P" were a proper name of that P, is necessarily false)

and (4**) with

> (4^p) Pa · the proposition expressed by $\ulcorner a$ has non-$P\urcorner$ where "a" is a proper name of a and "P" is a proper name of P, or the proposition which would

be expressed by $\ulcorner a$ has non-$P\urcorner$ if "a" were a
proper name of a and "P" were a proper name of
P, is necessarily false.

Both of these proposals have all of the advantages of our
first two de dicto reinterpretations and none of their disad-
vantages. After all, according to Kaplan's proposal, (7) is
interpreted as

(7^k) ($\exists \alpha$) [Denotes$_{nec.}$ (α, the number I am thinking
   about) and $\ulcorner \alpha$ is greater than seven$\urcorner$ is necessarily
   true],

which is, as any correct interpretation of (7) must be, true.
After all, "nine" does necessarily denote that number which
I am now thinking about, and "nine is greater than seven" is
necessarily true. On the other hand, according to Kaplan's
proposal, (8) is interpreted as

(8^k) ($\exists \alpha$) [Denotes$_{nec.}$ (α, nine) $\cdot \ulcorner \alpha$ is being thought
   about by me now$\urcorner$ is necessarily true],

which is, as any correct interpretation of (8) must be, false.
After all, although "nine" necessarily denotes nine, "nine is
being thought about by me now" is not necessarily true, and
although "the number I am thinking about now is being
thought about by me now" is necessarily true, "the number
I am thinking about now" does not necessarily name nine.
Similarly, according to Plantinga's theory, (7) is interpreted
as

(7^p) the number that I am now thinking of is greater
   than seven and the proposition expressed by $\ulcorner a$
   has non-$P\urcorner$, where "a" is a proper name of the
   number I am now thinking of and "P" is a proper
   name of the property of being greater than seven,
   or the proposition that would be expressed by $\ulcorner a$
   has non-$P\urcorner$ if "a" were a proper name of the number I am now thinking of and "P" were a proper
   name of the property of being greater than seven,
   is necessarily false

which is, as any correct interpretation of (7) must be, true. On the other hand, according to Plantinga's proposal, (8) is interpreted as

(8^p) nine is being thought about by me now and the proposition expressed by ⌜a has non-P⌝, where "a" is a proper name of nine, and "P" is a proper name of the property of being thought about by me now, or the proposition which would be expressed by ⌜a has non-P⌝ if "a" were a proper name of nine and "P" were a proper name of the property of being thought about by me now, is necessarily false.

which is, as any correct interpretation of (8) must be, false.

Intuitively, what has happened here is that Kaplan and Plantinga have modified (2**) and (4**) to place restrictions on the names involved in the de dicto reinterpretation of (2) and (4). The crucial idea behind these restrictions is to insure that the necessary truth of the relevant sentence of the form ⌜α is a P⌝ is *not* due merely to the meaning of the name used, where the name needn't name the object. If it were, then the sentence of the form ⌜α is a P⌝ might be a necessary truth, although the object in question might not necessarily have the property in question. Thus, although "the number I am thinking about now is being thought about by me now" is a necessary truth, its necessity is due to the meaning of the name "the number I am thinking about now," and that name needn't (and doesn't, in many worlds) name nine. As a result, the necessary truth of that sentence does *not* entail that the number in question, nine, necessarily has the property of being thought about by me now.

Plantinga accomplishes this goal by requiring the use of proper names for the objects and properties. While he doesn't say so, he presumably thinks that doing this will work because proper names only have reference and not any meaning. Kaplan accomplishes the same goal, while allowing names that have meanings, by requiring that the names, by virtue of their meaning, denote the same object in all possible worlds. Whichever way is adopted, one gets the desirable result that sentences like (8) are false.

There is another set of intuitions that lie behind these technical modifications, intuitions that may help explain why Kaplan and Plantinga chose the particular solutions that they did (rather than the solution offered by the other, for example). Suppose that one held the following views: (a) an object has a property essentially only if it has it in all possible worlds; (b) if an object does not exist in a given world, then it has no properties in that world. Then, in order for an object to have a property essentially, it would have to exist in all possible worlds and have that property in all possible worlds. This is, of course, precisely what follows according to Kaplan's de dicto reinterpretation. After all, a has P necessarily, according to Kaplan, only if there is some name α that denotes a in all possible worlds and which is such that $\ulcorner P\alpha\urcorner$ is necessarily true. Since α denotes a in all possible worlds, a must exist in all possible worlds. Given then the truth of $\ulcorner P\alpha\urcorner$ in all possible worlds, a must have P in all possible worlds. Suppose now that one holds (as does Plantinga) that it is sufficient for an object's having a property essentially that it have it in all worlds in which it exists. Then one would have to reject Kaplan's de dicto reinterpretation, which requires too much, and offer a different de dicto reinterpretation, like the one offered by Plantinga.

5.3 THE DIFFICULTIES WITH THE REINTERPRETATIONS

Let us first examine Kaplan's de dicto reinterpretation. There are, it seems to me, several major difficulties with it. First, by virtue of using the notion of denoting necessarily, Kaplan has not really translated all modal claims into de dicto claims, and has not therefore accomplished much by his reinterpretation. To see that this is so, consider the following variant of (8), which is also false:

(8′) the number I am thinking about now is essentially being thought about by me now.

Kaplan would transcribe this as

(8'$_k$) ($\exists\alpha$)[Denotes$_{nec.}$ (α, the number I am thinking about now). ⌜α is being thought about by me now⌝ is necessarily true]

Is this transcription true or false? It all depends upon what you mean by "denotes necessarily." If that merely means that "'the number I am thinking about now' denotes the number I am thinking about now" is necessarily true, then "the number I am thinking about now" necessarily denotes the number I am thinking about now. It would then follow that (8'^{k}) is true, and this is unacceptable. Kaplan himself realizes then that he must mean something else, and something that is not a de dicto necessity, by "denotes necessarily." But if so, what has he accomplished? Isn't he left with the de re notion of names having certain properties necessarily, viz. the property of naming certain objects? If that de re notion can be understood independently of a de dicto reinterpretation, why can't others? And if it cannot, then we do not understand Kaplan's de dicto reinterpretation that employs it. In short, then, Kaplan's de dicto reinterpretation is either unnecessary or unsuccessful.

Second, Kaplan's reinterpretation carries with it certain unfortunate ontological commitments. After all, for Kaplan, an object has a property essentially only if there exists a name for that object that necessarily denotes it. Intuitively, this is unsatisfactory because the truth of the essentialist claim seems to be independent of the existence of names. Why should the truth of the claim that nine is necessarily greater than seven depend upon the existence of a name for nine? No doubt, this objection seems less serious if one thinks of names just as abstract shapes and if one believes that these abstract shapes, like all abstract objects, must exist necessarily. But these are strong ontological views, and it seems wiser to reject a reinterpretation that requires the acceptance of such strong claims.

Third, there are straightforward counterexamples to Kaplan's analysis, counterexamples that are due to the fact that Kaplan has imposed no restrictions upon the ways in which you can specify the property in the relevant de dicto claim.

Consider as a true claim in our above examples, that

(9) nine is necessarily identical with that number which I am thinking about now.

[That (9) is true can be seen when it is contrasted with (8)]. According to Kaplan, (9) is to be equivalent to

(9^k) ($\exists\alpha$) [Denotes$_{nec.}$ (α, nine). $\ulcorner\alpha$ = that number which I am thinking about now$\urcorner$ is necessarily true]

which is false both for "nine" (since the resulting sentence is not necessarily true) and for "that number which I am thinking about now" (since it does not necessarily denote nine).

Fourth, Kaplan is forced to deny that people (or chairs, or trees) have even the most seemingly unproblematic essential properties. After all, if nothing else, we would surely want to say that Jones is necessarily identical with himself. According to Kaplan's analysis, not even this is true of Jones. It is easy to see what has gone wrong here. Kaplan has, in effect, required that an object have a property in all possible worlds, and not merely in all possible worlds in which the object exists, in order for the object to have it necessarily. Now since, for any concrete object, there are possible worlds in which it does not exist, it follows that it does not have any property in all possible worlds and that, according to Kaplan's approach, it does not have any property necessarily. It should be noted, to be fair to Kaplan, that he can allow for the necessity of the law of identity and for Jones's being identical with Jones. These claims are, after all, just

(10) necessarily, for all x, x is identical with x

and

(11) necessarily, Jones is identical with Jones

and, by all accounts, they can be understood as

(10′) "for all x, x is identical with x" is necessarily true and as

(11′) "Jones is identical with Jones" is necessarily true.

But neither of these claims attributes to Jones, or to all objects, the property of being necessarily self-identical. The claims that do that are

(12) for all x, x is necessarily identical with x

and

(13) Jones is necessarily identical with Jones,

and these true claims are, unfortunately for Kaplan, false according to his reinterpretation of them. They are, after all, according to Kaplan, equivalent to

(12^k) $(x)(\exists \alpha)$ [Denotes$_{nec.}$ (α, x) ⌜α is identical with x⌝ is necessarily true]

and

(13^k) $(\exists \alpha)$ [Denotes$_{nec.}$ $(\alpha,$ Jones) · ⌜α is identical with Jones⌝ is necessarily true],

and these are clearly false.

Plantinga's de dicto reinterpretation avoids all of the above objections. Because he does not use the notion of necessary naming, he has not smuggled in that de re element into his de dicto account. Because he can handle cases in which the object lacks a name, he has not smuggled in any undesirable ontological commitments to names. Because he has imposed restrictions upon the ways in which the property is specified in the relevant de dicto claims, his reading of (9), which is

(9^P) nine is identical with that number which I am thinking about now, and the proposition expressed by ⌜a has non-P⌝, where "a" is a proper name of nine and "P" is a proper name of the property of being identical with that number which I am thinking about now, or the proposition which would be expressed by ⌜*a* has non-*P*⌝ if "*a*" were a proper name of nine and "*P*" were a proper name of the property of being identical with that number which I am thinking about now, is necessarily false

is true, as any proper analysis of (9) must be. Finally, because he only requires that an object have a property in all worlds in which it exists in order to have the property necessarily, he can allow for the unproblematic truth of such claims as (12) and (13). Claim (13), for example, is analyzed as

(13ᴾ) Jones is identical with Jones, and the proposition expressed by ⌜*a* has non-*P*⌝, where "*a*" is a proper name of Jones and "*P*" is a proper name of the property of being identical with Jones, or the proposition which would be expressed by ⌜*a* has non-*P*⌝ if "*a*" were a proper name of Jones and "*P*" were a proper name of the property of being identical with Jones, is necessarily false,

and (13ᴾ) is, as it should be, true.

Despite these advantages, Plantinga's theory fails, I believe, to be helpful for our problem. After all, our problem was to find a way of understanding de re essentialist claims, and our hope was that these de dicto reinterpretations would enable us to understand de re modalities without any reference to the problematic notion of identity across possible worlds. It seems, however, that Plantinga's analysis uses that very notion of identity across possible worlds.

To see that this is so, we must look more carefully at Plantinga's analysis of propositions of the form ⌜*a* has *P* necessarily⌝, which came to

(4ᴾ) *Pa* and the proposition expressed by ⌜*a* has non-*P*⌝ where "*a*" is the proper name of *a* and "*P*" is the proper name of *P*, or the proposition which would be expressed by ⌜*a* has non-*P*⌝ if "*a*" were a proper name of *a* and "*P*" were a proper name of *P*, is necessarily false.

What does it mean to say that the proposition in question is necessarily false? It means, presumably, that it is false in all possible worlds. If a certain proposition is false in all possible worlds, then a has P necessarily. But, of course, it must be the same proposition which is false in all possible worlds. Then, only, can we say that that proposition is necessarily false. So Plantinga's analysis already involves the notion of trans-world identity, at least insofar as it applies to propositions.

In truth, Plantinga himself has pointed out that any real problems about understanding the de re claims are equally present in understanding de dicto claims. As he says:

> An object has a given property essentially just in case it couldn't conceivably have lacked that property; a proposition is necessarily true, just in case it couldn't conceivably have been false. Is the latter more limpid than the former? Is it harder to understand the claim that Socrates could have been a planet than the claim that the proposition *Socrates is a planet* could have been true? . . . I therefore do not see that modality de re is in principle more obscure than modality de dicto.[7]

Plantinga himself is not worried, because, as we have seen, he thinks that there is no problem about cross-world identity. If we are right, however, in our argument that there is a problem of cross-world identity, then we must conclude that both de re and de dicto claims are problematic.

There is, I believe, an even more fundamental objection to Plantinga's approach. It seems to me that it cannot provide, without metaphysical extravagance, for a proper ontological basis for essentialism. To see why this is so, let us look at a typical essentialist claim concerning a merely contingently existing object, the claim that

(14)   Baruch Brody is essentially a person.

For Plantinga, the truth of this claim consists in Baruch Brody's having the property of being a person in all worlds in which he exists (for it is this that makes the relevant proposition which asserts that he is not a person necessarily false). I want to argue that this is an inadequate ontological base, and it cannot be made adequate.

There has been, in recent years, considerable debate about the ontological status of possible worlds and the possibilities in them.[8] In order to make the case as favorable as possible for people like Plantinga, I shall just assume here that these worlds and the possibilities in them exist, although they are not actual. Even if one holds this extreme realist view, one still must, I submit, ground the existence or nonexistence of possibilities in the actual. One must, at least, unless one is prepared to adopt an indexical theory of actuality and assign no special status to the actual as opposed to the merely possible. To avoid the metaphysical extravagance of this "indexical theory of actuality," one grounds the existence of possible worlds and possibilities in the conditions of the actual world. This is what the special status of the actual comes to. Now, I fail to see how approaches like Plantinga's do this for claims like (14). What, in the actuality of Baruch Brody, is the foundation for the nonexistence of any world in which, from the very beginning, Baruch Brody was other than a person?

Let me elaborate on this last point. In a world in which Baruch Brody exists, and exists as a person, that actuality serves as the ontological foundation of the fact that there are no possible futures in that world in which he continues to exist, but not as person. His actual personhood in that world determines that all of his future possibilities in that world are person-possibilities. But if we are envisaging, as Plantinga is, a wider variety of possible worlds, what, in the actual, serves as the ontological foundation for there being no possible world in which, from the very beginning, Baruch Brody was not a person? How can his actual condition in this world ground what he might have been like in some possible world in which he was very different from the beginning of his existence?

Two themes emerge from this investigation of Kaplan's and Plantinga's suggestions. The first is that it is harder than it initially seems to do away with the de re nature of essentialist claims. De dicto interpretations often contain disguised de re elements. We would probably do better, therefore, to try to find meaning for the de re independently of the de dicto. That is what we will be doing in the next section. Second, whatever theory we find interesting must also be examined for its ontological implications.

5.4 IDENTITY ACROSS POSSIBLE WORLDS

To say that an object a has a property P essentially is to say that it has P and that in all of certain worlds (all possible, all in which something identical with it exists, . . .), the object identical with it has P. This is the standard interpretation of de re essentialist claims. This interpretation assumes that meaning has been given to the claim that an object x in a world w is identical with a in the actual world. What, however, is the meaning of this cross-world identity? This is the problem that we put aside at the end of Section 5.1 and to which we must now return in light of the failure of the de dicto reinterpretations. In this section, we will first consider the solutions that have been offered by Chisholm and Lewis. We will then consider the claim that Kripke's work has shown that there really is no problem. We will finally discuss two solutions to the problem, one if one wants a Plantinga-like theory, and one if one wants to base one's theory on the type of Aristotelean essentialism that we introduced in Chapter Four of this book. We shall show that only the latter works.

Chisholm Solutions and Lewis Solutions

Chisholm has suggested that the problem of identity across possible worlds can be solved if we adopt a certain supposition, viz. that for every object, there is a set of properties which it has in all possible worlds and which is had by no other object in any possible worlds.[9] Given this supposition, we could easily solve the problem of identity across possible worlds. Consider object a. It has, according to our supposition, some uniquely held properties, it has them in all possible worlds, and it has them uniquely in all possible worlds. Let those properties be P. Then, in any given world, an object x in that world is identical with a in the actual world just in case x has P.

The trouble with this suggestion is with its initial supposition. Indeed, for ordinary objects like chairs and people, the supposition looks very implausible. Consider, on the one hand, properties they have uniquely, like coming into existence at a certain spatiotemporal point. These are properties that they probably don't have in all possible worlds (not even in all of those in which they exist). Without that crucial interrupting telephone call, for example, I and the chair I am sitting on would have been created just a bit earlier (and if there were no such call, there could have been one). Even if Babe Ruth was the first player to hit sixty home runs, he might never have played baseball. And so on. It is hard to see that there are any uniquely held properties had by such objects that are had by them in all possible worlds. Even those properties that have figured so prominently in theories of identity don't fit the bill. I may be the unique person who has the particular set of beliefs, feelings, memories, and traits that I do, but I certainly might have had a very different set (just suppose, for example, that at birth I had been adopted by very different parents). Consider, on the other hand, properties that they might plausibly be held to have in all possible worlds (or even in only those in which they exist). It might be plausible to hold, for example, that person a is a person in all possible worlds (or, at least, in all in which a exists). Person a is, however, not uniquely a person; there are, at least in this world (and presumably many others), many people. And so on. None of this is, of course, a proof that Chisholm's supposition is in error; it does, however, suggest that it is in real trouble.

It might be thought that there are objects, like numbers and propositions, about which Chisholm's supposition is plausible. Four, it might be suggested, is the only object in any world which is the sum of two and two, and it is the sum of two and two in all possible worlds. The proposition that

four is the sum of two and two is the only object in any
world which is the contradictory of the proposition that four
is not the sum of two and two, and it is its contradictory in
all possible worlds. Even if this suggestion is accepted,
however, it will not help solve our problem about identity
across possible worlds. The relevant properties involve
other objects, and we solve the problem of identity for any
given object only by raising the problem of identity for some
other object. To be told that x in some world is identical with
four in our world just in case x, in that world, is the sum of
the object in that world identical with our number two and
the object in that world identical with our number two is not
at all helpful. We are in the beginnings of an infinite (circular, I suspect) regress.

There is one final point that should be noted about
Chisholm's suggestion. There is, for all possible objects, at
least one property that satisfies the supposition. For example, only Baruch Brody has the property of-being-Baruch-
Brody (which is, of course, different from the property of
being self-identical, a widely held property), and he has it in
all possible worlds. A similar property exists, presumably,
for every object. But none of this will help Chisholm. The
identity property in question is a cross-world identity property. It must be if Baruch Brody in some other world is to
have it. And it will certainly do no good to define cross-
world identity in terms of cross-world identity.

A very different solution to the problem of cross-world
identity has been proposed by David Lewis.[10] He suggests
dropping all talk about identity across possible worlds. According to him, an object has a property essentially just in
case it has the property in the actual world and its counterparts in all possible worlds (or at least, in all in which it has a
counterpart) also have the property. The counterpart(s) in
some possible world of an object a in the actual world is the
object(s) in the possible world that resemble a sufficiently
and that are such that nothing else in that world resembles a
more.

In light of our previous discussion, it is easy to see what

Lewis is up to. Lewis recognizes that, given the variety of possible worlds in which (intuitively) we exist, there aren't many properties that we have in all of them, and the ones that there are are had by too many objects to be of any use for defining cross-world identity. He proposes, instead, to look at resembling objects, objects that might resemble us in different ways. This way, he doesn't have to worry about the property being had by us in *all* the possible worlds. On this proposal, the properties we have essentially are determined by the properties had in the possible worlds by those resembling objects. And for technical reasons, he has to allow for the possibility that there might be more than one of them in a given possible world; this leads him to give up identity-talk and to talk instead about counterparts.

Fred Feldman and Alvin Plantinga have raised substantial technical objections to Lewis's proposal.[11] I should like, however, to raise a different sort of difficulty. Lewis himself notes that the major weakness in his account is the difficulty of providing an adequate measure of resemblance. One thing, however, is certain; resemblance is *not* simply a question of the number of properties had in common. Resemblance in certain respects is obviously going to have to count more than resemblance in other respects. For example, it is far more important, in determining if I have a counterpart in some world w, that the candidate be a person than that the candidate be sitting in the chair in which I am sitting in now. Unless, as Lewis himself notes, we weigh various resemblances differently, we will get the wrong type of theory. I should like to suggest that the properties to be weighed most are the very properties that are intuitively essential; if this does not happen, then it would be an amazing coincidence if the theory gave intuitively acceptable results. All of this suggests that Lewis's program is not very promising. Something analogous to a theory of essentialism is probably needed in order to develop an adequate theory of resemblance, and any approach that wants to use the latter to develop the former is in very serious trouble.

Has Kripke Eliminated the Need for a Solution?

It is widely believed that Kripke's work on the use of proper names as rigid designators has undercut the problem of identity across possible worlds, and that essentialist talk as well as counterfactual talk can be explained without any reference to that notion of identity. [12] The source of this belief is Kripke himself, who says,

> those who have argued that to make sense of the notion of rigid designator, we must antecedently make sense of "criteria of transworld identity" have precisely reversed the cart and the horse; it is because we can refer (rigidly) to Nixon, and stipulate that we are speaking of what might have happened to him (under certain circumstances), that "transworld identifications" are unproblematic in such cases. [13]

At another point, Kripke says,

> "Possible worlds" are stipulated, not discovered by powerful telescopes. There is no reason why we cannot stipulate that, in talking about what would have happened to Nixon in a certain counter-factual situation, we are talking about what would have happened to him. [14]

What is a rigid designator and why is it supposed that rigid designators can remove the need for solving the problem of identity? To say that a designator is rigid is to say that it designates the same object in all other possible worlds and all other counterfactual situations as it does in the actual world. The idea is that the designation for all possible worlds is determined by the designation in the actual world. Kripke feels that proper names, but not most descriptions, are rigid designators. We can leave for other occasions the truth of that claim; all that we need for now is a conviction that at least some designators do designate rigidly. The question then is why the existence of these designators removes the need for solving the problem of trans-world identity.

The best way to understand Kripke's point is to think of it this way: we claimed, at the beginning of this section, that ⌜a has P essentially⌝ *means* that a has P and that in all worlds containing an object identical with a, that object has P. On this account, the meaningfulness of essentialist claims presupposes the meaningfulness of trans-world identity. But suppose we simply said that ⌜a has P essentially⌝ *means* that a has P and that in all worlds containing a, a has P. This account makes no reference to cross-world identity and does provide an account of the meaning of essentialist claims. But can we offer this account? Can we use a name which refers to some object in the actual world to refer to that object in some possible world? If Kripke is right, and the name in question is a rigid designator, it seems to follow that we can, and that by doing so we avoid any need to employ the notion of trans-world identity.

It is quite understandable that this suggestion of Kripke's has been so favorably received. I should like to suggest, however, that it really doesn't work, and that rigidity of designation really does presuppose cross-world identity. I would like to develop my argument by comparing designation of objects in other possible worlds with designation of objects at other possible times.

In the first part of the book, we argued that there was no objection to taking as primitive names for objects that endured through time. With such names, we had, of course, no difficulty in talking about the past and the future, and it even turned out that we could use such names in offering a simple theory of identity through time. Kripke's suggestion is very similar to that. We are to begin by taking as primitive names for objects that persist through possible worlds. With such names, we will have no difficulty in talking about possibilities and about counterfactual situations, and perhaps we could then use such names in offering a theory of identity across possible worlds.

My argument against Kripke is that there is an important disanalogy between these cases, and as a result of this disanalogy, there are reasons why we can take names of temporally enduring objects as primitive, but we must introduce names for objects that persist through possible worlds on the basis of a definition of cross-world identity. The argument runs in outline as follows: at least some of the objects that we perceive do endure through time and do persist through possible worlds. However, while we perceive their endurance through time, we do not perceive their persistence through possible worlds. It is because we can perceive their endurance through time that we can take names for enduring objects as primitive. Because we cannot perceive their persistence through possible worlds, names for persisting objects must be constructed from names for nonpersisting objects by use of a definition of cross-world identity. Each of these steps require further elaboration, which we shall now provide.

The chair in front of me, which I am looking at now, was here yesterday and will be here tomorrow. In that way, some of the objects that we perceive do endure through time. The chair is blue, but it might well have been red. In that way, some of the objects that we perceive do persist through possible worlds. To be sure, we may at the same time perceive temporal stages of the chair that do not endure through time and worldly stages of the chair that do not persist through possible worlds. But that does not, of course, take away from the truth of the first premise of our argument.

I saw my chair yesterday and will see it tomorrow. In this way, we perceive the endurance of enduring objects. However, while I can see that my chair is blue, I cannot see (in the perceptual sense) that it might have been red. In this way, we cannot perceive the persistence of persisting objects. This is all that is meant by the second premise of the argument, and these claims seem to be straightforwardly true.

Before turning to the third and crucial step, we must say a bit more about the relation between what we have just said and some claims we advanced in Chapter Two when talking about the constructionist's program. At a certain point in our argument in Chapter Two, we conceded the possibility that we first believe of the first objects of our knowledge that they are momentary objects. The thing to note is that that concession is perfectly compatible with our argument here. We may see the chair yesterday and see it tomorrow and still believe of it that it is a momentary object. All that is required for this is that we not realize that the chair seen tomorrow is identical with the chair seen yesterday.

We turn now to the crucial third step of the argument. The basic idea behind the third step is just this: we should accept, as a constraint on the construction of metaphysically satisfactory reconstructions, the requirement that primitive names be independently learnable (that we be able to acquire knowledge of their referent independently of acquiring knowledge of the referent of other names). Now, in the case of names that are names for enduring objects, they are independently learnable. We acquire knowledge of the referent of the name by hearing it repeated at different times, by seeing similarities in the environment of those times, and so on. Through this process, the details of which are not completely known at this time, we assign as the referent of the name the enduring object whose endurance we are perceiving. But can we do the same thing with names for persisting objects? My claim is that we cannot, and that we have to acquire the referent of a persisting name by first learning names for enduring objects and then constructing names for persisting objects out of names for enduring objects and a definition of cross-world identity. We cannot precisely because independently learning the referent of persisting names requires our perceiving the persistence (and not merely the persisting object), and we do not perceive the persistence. Therefore, since names for persisting objects are not independently learnable, they should not be taken as primitive.

Our picture then is this: looking in front of me, I perceive an object that is enduring and persisting. I also perceive its temporal stage and its worldly stage. The latter is an enduring but not persisting object. Names for it can be primitive because I can learn their referent without having to know the referent of other names. I can do this because I can perceive the endurance of what I am perceiving. But names for objects that both endure and persist cannot be primitive in our system because the referent of such a name is not independently learnable. The referent can only be learned by referring to it by use of names for enduring nonpersistent objects and an account of cross-world identity. In short, ''Joe'' is first a name for Joe's worldly stage, and can only later become a name for Joe. Identity across possible worlds is prior to rigid designation, and we must, therefore, resume our search for a definition of that identity.

In presenting the argument against Kripke, I have assumed that there is, for any given enduring and persisting object, a nonenduring and nonpersisting temporal stage and an enduring but nonpersisting worldly stage. Making this assumption simplified our argument. The argument does not, however, rest on that assumption. We could run it without that assumption as follows: the objects that we perceive do endure through time and do persist through possible worlds. However, although we perceive their endurance through time, we do not perceive their persistence through possible worlds. Because this is so, although we can learn without any definition of identity across time to use names for these objects at later times than when we first acquired the name, we can only learn to use these names to refer to the object in other possible worlds through a definition of cross-world identity. Notice three things about this version of the argument: (1) it is exactly like the initial argument except for its third step; (2) the new third step makes no reference to any objects other than the enduring and persisting objects; (3) the rationale for the new third step is really very analogous to the rationale for the old third step—explicit definition plays a role because of the limitation of experience. In the end, then, whatever our ontology, identity across possible worlds is prior to rigid designation. Our ontology only determines whether, without a definition of identity, we only have names for nonpersisting objects or we have names for persisting objects but do not know how to use them to talk about other possible worlds.

A Plantinga-like Solution

This difficulty also rules out a suggested solution to the problem of identity across possible worlds. Several people have suggested that my way of solving the problem of identity through time could be generalized to solve the problem of identity across possible worlds. Let me briefly explain this suggestion, show why it would lead to a Plantinga-like solution, and then show why our criticism of Kripke undercuts this suggestion.

The question before us is to explain when a in world w_1 is identical with b in w_2. Why can't we say that they are identical if they have all of their properties in common? Intuitively, it might seem as though we could not. After all, a in world w_1 might have different properties from b in w_2 and still be identical with b (this is, after all, the point of possible worlds). But this intuition is in error. We are saying that:

$$a = b =_{\text{def}} (P)\ (w)\ (t)\ (P_{atw} \equiv P_{btw}).$$

In other words, "$a = b$" means that for any given time and any given world, a has P at that time in that world if and only if b has P at that time *in that world*.

An example will bring out the point. An object a in w_1 at t_1 has property P, while an object b in w_2 at t_1 has property not-P. This definition of identity allows them to be identical. They will be identical, of course, only if (among other things) a in w_2 at t_1 has not-P and b in w_1 at t_1 has P, but this is perfectly possible.

What is happening here is very similar to what we said about identity through time in Chapter One. An object a at t_1 is identical with b at t_2 if they have the same properties at the same times, and they need not have the same properties at different times. Similarly, an object in w_1 is identical with an object in w_2 if they have the same properties at the same times in the same worlds, and they need not have the same properties in different possible worlds.

The suggestion then is that indiscernibility, properly understood, can be used as a definition even of identity across possible worlds. What type of theory of essentialism does this provide? Well, one thing to note is that it allows a in w_1 to be identical with b in w_2 even if they have been very different from the very beginning of their existence. This allows, in effect, for the sort of theory which, as we saw in Section 5.3, is envisaged in Plantinga's theory.

As attractive as this suggestion might seem, it will not do. In order for this account of identity to work, we must have available names of persisting objects. This enables us to say that a, an object in w_1, has in w_2 the same properties that b, an object in w_2, has in w_2, and that b has in w_1 the same properties that a has in w_1. But we have argued against Kripke that names for persisting objects presuppose cross-world identity, and if that argument is correct, it follows that such names cannot be used in defining cross-world identity. Therefore, this suggestion will not work.

None of this should come as a surprise. We can, as is required by our definition, use names for enduring objects in defining identity across time only because such names can be primitive. Since names for persisting objects cannot be primitive, we cannot use them in defining cross-world identity as indiscernibility properly understood.

A similar difficulty arises for the proposal of moderate Haecceitism put forward by Professor Robert Adams in a very important recent article. [15] This position consists of the following two claims: first, trans-world identity and thisnesses (the property of being identical with a certain particular individual) are primitive; and second, there are logical connections between possessing a certain thisness and possessing certain suchnesses. This position would, of course, avoid the problem of defining trans-world identity by treating it as primitive. The trouble is that it will have to take a property such as the property of-being-identical-with-object-o as primitive, and that requires names for persisting objects as primitive. If we are right that such names cannot be primitive, then Adams's proposal will not do.

An Aristotelean Solution

In Section 4.2, we put forward a theory of essentialism according to which an object *a* had a property *P* essentially just in case *a* has *P* and *a*'s losing *P* would mean *a*'s going out of existence. According to that theory, *a* has a property *P* accidentally just if *a* can lose it without going out of existence. The question that we now have to consider is whether such a theory can deal with the problem of identity across possible worlds.

It might seem that such a theory doesn't have to deal with the whole problem. After all, the problem arose only because we explained "*a* has *P* essentially" as meaning "*a* has *P*, and in all worlds in which there is something identical with *a*, that thing has *P*." But if we explain the meaning of "*a* has *P* essentially" simply in terms of "*a* has *P* and cannot lose *P* without going out of existence," then perhaps the whole problem disappears. After all, there seems to be no reference in the analysans to cross-world identity.

Unfortunately, this short way out of the problem won't do. The analysans contain the phrase "cannot lose *P* without going out of existence" and that sounds like "there is no world containing a *b* identical with it in which *b* continues to exist after losing *P*," so the analysans do contain cross-world identity in an implicit fashion.

Although this Aristotelean theory cannot, therefore, avoid in this easy way the problem of cross-world identity, it is in a unique position to avoid that problem anyway. The clue to this is to be found in the following passage by David Kaplan:

> When the worlds have a common part, as when we are considering alternative futures to the present, the individual(s) can be traced back to the common part by the usual continuity conditions and there compared. But for individuals not extant during an overlap, such techniques are unavailing. It seems that such radically disjointed worlds are sometimes contemplated by modal logicians.[16]

What Kaplan failed to realize is that, whatever may or may not be contemplated by modal logicians, all that is needed to explain essentialist claims in our Aristotelean framework is the idea of alternative futures to the present. Let me explain.

The intuitive idea is this: if a can lose P and still exist, if the loss of P would be a mere alteration, then there is a possible future in which a continues to exist but does not have P. On the other hand, if a cannot lose P without going out of existence, if the loss of P is a passing-away of a, then there is no possible future in which a continues to exist but does not have P. So, we can as Aristoteleans say that "a has P essentially" means "a has P and there is no possible future in which a continues to exist but does not have P," while "a has P accidentally," means "a has P and there is a possible future in which a continues to exist without having P." The only notion of identity involved here is that of identity across time, and we have, therefore, an explanation of essentialism.

This last point needs some elaboration. What is being envisaged here is a shrub whose base is the present and whose branches are the possible futures (Figure 3). What we need to treat as identical is a and a', a and a'', a and a''', and so on. We can then say that if one of a', a'', a''', . . . doesn't have P and still exists, then a only has P accidentally. But the identity of a and a', a and a'', a and a''', . . . only requires the notion of identity across time, and that can, in light of our results in Chapter One, be taken as unproblematic. To be

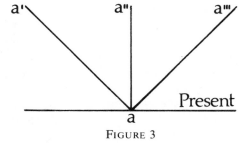

FIGURE 3

sure, in order to preserve transitivity of identity, we want a' to be identical with a'', . . . but that can be done simply by adding that possible future objects x and y are identical with each other if they are identical with the same present object.

We can conclude our long discussion of identity across possible worlds with the realization that the Aristotelean approach to essentialism, alone among theories of essentialism, has dealt with that problem and given content to essentialist claims. In the next few sections, we will develop this theory in much fuller detail.

5.5 THE DEVELOPMENT OF ARISTOTELEAN ESSENTIALISM (I)

The theory that we have presented so far says that "a has P essentially" means "a has P and there is no possible future in which a continues to exist but does not have P." As we shall see shortly, this theory needs to be modified and expanded upon in a number of ways.

The first difficulty that we have to consider is caused by what might be called after-effect properties. Consider, for example, the property of-having-sired-children. I have that property, and there is no possible future in which I continue to exist but do not have that property. Having sired children, I cannot lose the property of-having-sired-children. It would seem to follow, on the account we have offered so far, that I have the property of-having-sired-children essentially. Intuitively, however, this is not satisfactory. It hardly seems necessary that I have that property.

There are a number of ways of dealing with this problem: (1) John Hooker has suggested[17] that we confine the distinction between essential and accidental properties to local properties, to properties whose attribution at any one time speaks only to what the world is like at that time. Since the attribution of the property of-having-sired-children speaks to what the world is like at some other time (the time, for example, at which I sired them), the property in question is neither essential nor accidental; (2) I acquired the property of having sired children at some point in time. Before then, I existed but did not have that property. We could, therefore, modify our definition to require that *a* has *P*, that *a* has always had *P* since it existed, and that there is no possible future in which *a* continues to exist but does not have *P*. With this modification, the property of-having-sired-children would be an accidental property; (3) there was some moment in the past at which I existed and at which there was a possible future in which I did not have any children and never acquired the property of-having-sired-children. We could, therefore, modify our definition even further to require that *a* has *P*, that *a* has always had *P* since it existed, and that, for any moment at which *a* has *P*, there is no possible future in which *a* continues to exist but does not have *P*. With this even stronger modification, the property of-having-sired-children would certainly be an accidental property.

The first of these three accounts seems to me to be unacceptable. This is due, in part, to its counterintuitive result that the property of-having-sired-children is neither essential nor accidental. It seems that we want to say that it is accidental (I might not have sired children and then I would not have the property), and it is a virtue of (2) and (3) that they lead to that result. Its unacceptability is also due, however, to the way in which it rules out certain essential properties as being neither essential nor accidental. If, as seems plausible, I am essentially a person, it would seem that I also have the property-of-having-been-born essentially. And yet, on Hooker's account, this property is neither essential nor accidental. Again, it is a virtue of (2) and (3) that they lead to the proper result that that property is an essential property.

Let us look more carefully at the second and third of these alternatives. It is important, to begin with, to understand the difference between them. We might represent them pictorially with trees, as in Figures 4 and 5. (2) requires that *a* have *P* from when it came into existence until now, and that it have it in all of its present possible futures. (3) requires that *a* have *P* from when it came into existence until now,

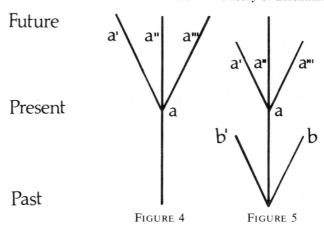

Future

Present

Past

FIGURE 4   FIGURE 5

and that it have it in all of the possible futures it has ever had or has. It should be noted that neither of these modifications of our original theory, despite their further requirements, poses any problem of identity across possible worlds. (2) only adds the identity of a with itself in the past, and that does not involve identity across possible worlds. (3) Only adds the identity of past possible future a's (b, b') with a in the past, and that is no more problematic than the identity of a with its present possible futures (a', a'', a''').

It is not too hard to construct examples which indicate that (3) is a better proposal than (2). Consider, for example, the property of-either-not-being-married-or-not-having-married-until-18 and a person Joe, who in fact does not marry until now, when he is 18. It seems not unreasonable to say that Joe has had that property since he existed, that he has it now, and that there is no possible future in which he continues to exist but lacks that property. On account (2), then, Joe has that property essentially. But that hardly seems intuitively satisfactory. The possession of this property hardly seems necessary; (3) yields the correct result. At some earlier time, say when Joe was 6, he had the property in question but there was (at that time) a possible future in which he lacked the property while continuing to exist (this would be a future in which he married at 17). So, on account (3), Joe only has the property accidentally, and this seems satisfactory.

But even the adoption of (3) is unsatisfactory. Consider the property of-coming-into-existence-in-Metuchen and a person Joe, who has that property. Joe has that property, has always had it since he existed, and there is no moment of time at which he had the property and at which there was a possible future in which he continued to exist without having that property. So even on account (3), Joe has that property essentially. And this seems, once more, intuitively unsatisfactory. Such a property seems accidental, and (3) is therefore unsatisfactory. (3), in fact, turns lots of accidents about your birth into essential properties, and we need to find a way to avoid this.

Kripke has suggested that certain properties about the origin of a person (that is, the property of having certain parents) are essential properties of that person. Without entering now into the legitimacy of that claim, I think that he would agree that not all are, and our problem is how to avoid this on our account. Do we have to accept as a consequence of our theory that the property of-having-coming-into-existence-in-Metuchen is an essential property of Joe?

It might be suggested that we ought to accept this conclusion, and perhaps even the earlier conclusions that the properties of having-sired-children or the property of either-not-being-married-or-not-having-married-until-18 are essential properties of all objects that have them at all. This suggestion is brought to mind by a remark of Kripke in a different context:

> One should not confuse the type of essence involved in the question ''What properties must an object retain if it is not to cease to exist, and what properties of the object can change while the object endures?'', which is a temporal question, with the question ''What (timeless) properties could the object not have failed to have and what properties could it have lacked while still

(timelessly) existing?'', which concerns necessity and not time and which is our topic here. [18]

The suggestion is this: our theory is a theory of the first type of essentialism, and these properties are essential given that first type of essentialism. We intuitively think that these properties are accidental because we are thinking of the second type of essentialism (we ask such questions as, "couldn't I have failed to sire children, have married before 18, and have come into existence elsewhere?"). Once we distinguish these two types of essentialism, we can accept without any hesitation the consequences of the initial statement of our theory, viz. that all of these properties are essential properties.

I cannot accept this suggestion. As I argued in the last section, the second type of essentialism involves a notion of cross-world identity to which we cannot give content. This means that only the first type of essentialism is available to us. Now, to be sure, we could accept it in its earliest formulation with all of its counterintuitive results. Doing so, however, would result in accepting a notion of little interest to us. What I want to show is that the first type of essentialism can be modified so as to yield intuitively satisfactory results, so as to yield a theory that corresponds to our intuitions about the necessary properties of objects. The adoption of (3) has led us closer to our goal, and I believe that we can meet even our latest counterexample.

Suppose that we consider the following structure in Figure 6. What this represents pictorially is the following definition: "*a* has property *P* essentially" means "*a* has *P*, *a* has always had *P* since *a* existed, and there is no moment of time at which *a* has had *P* and at which there is a possible future (past) in which *a* continues to exist (existed) without *P*." In other words, in order for *a* to have *P* essentially, there must be no possible past, as well as no possible future, in which *a* exists without *P*. Given this definition, our problem disappears. Joe only has the property of coming-into-existence-in-Metuchen accidentally, because there are possible pasts

Future

Present

Past

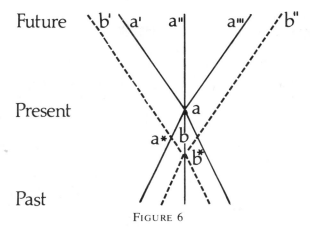

FIGURE 6

(for instance, where his parents were elsewhere) in which he existed without that property.

There are a number of things that ought to be noted about this latest account: (1) Like our earlier definitions, it does not introduce any special notions of cross-world identity. We have, of course, the identity of a with b earlier on, but that is just a matter of identity through time. The identity of a with its possible futures (such as a') and its possible pasts (a^*) is also a matter of identity through time, and this is also true of the identity of b with its possible futures (b') and its possible pasts (b^*). To be sure, in order to preserve the transitivity of identity, we want all these possible future objects and possible past objects to be identical with each other, but this can be done by adding that possible future and past objects are identical with each other if they are identical with the same present or past object. As Kaplan had already seen in the passage quoted above, we have no problem of identity across possible worlds so long as they overlap. (2) The introduction of possible pasts does differ from the introduction of possible futures. It blurs, for example, an ontological distinction that many feel between the past and the future. It seems to many that the future is open, and involves real possibilities, while the past is closed and settled. Our earlier definitions of essentialism preserved this feeling by introducing possible futures while not introducing possible pasts. This current definition does eliminate this assymetry. It seems to me, however, that if we talk about whether certain properties that have implications for the past (such as the property of coming-into-existence-in-Metuchen) are essential or accidental, we must introduce considerations about possible alternative pasts; moreover, as long as we understand that these are closed possibilities, as long as we understand that these are possibilities whose nonactuality is settled, I cannot see any objections to our introducing these possible pasts. (3) There is another important difference between possible pasts and possible futures. A possible future is any future whose existence is logically compatible with the existence of the actual present. But a possible past is not a past whose existence is logically compatible with the existence of the actual present. If it were, there could be no possible past in which I came into existence in some place other than Metuchen, since one of my current properties is that of-having-come-into-existence-in-Metuchen. What is needed here is this consideration: we introduce possible pasts when considering whether a certain property is had by a certain object essentially or accidentally. For consideration of that question, a possible past is a past whose existence is logically compatible with the existence of the actual present (where we exclude from the description of the actual present the statement that that object has that property and any other statement that entails it). (4) A possible past for some earlier actual past moment is also a possible past for the actual present moment. This immediately gives rise to a simplification of our modal diagram. We can represent that simplification as in Figure 7. Can we get rid of the remaining dotted lines? They represent possible futures of actual past moments and were needed to deal with certain counterexamples. There seems to be no way of dealing with them otherwise. We can, therefore, simplify our definition of essentialism to capture what is represented in

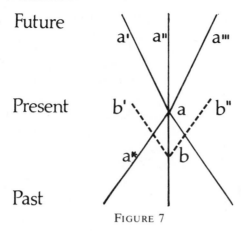

Future

Present

Past

FIGURE 7

Figure 7 by saying that "*a* has property *P* essentially" means "*a* has *P*, *a* has always had *P*, there is no possible past in which *a* exists without *P*, and there is no moment of time at which *a* has had *P* and at which there is a possible future in which *a* exists without *P*." We cannot, however, simplify it further by modifying the last clause to read simply "there is no possible future in which *a* exists without *P*."

To summarize, then, we have in this section shown how the Aristotelean theory of essentialism, the only one that seems capable of providing the concept of identity which is needed to make sense of essentialist claims, can be developed so as to capture most of our intuitions about which properties are had essentially by objects. What is important is that we can do this by merely considering alternatives based upon an actual present.

5.6   THE DEVELOPMENT OF ARISTOTELEAN ESSENTIALISM (II)

In this section, I want to develop more fully the Aristotelean aspects of our theory of essentialism. I want, to begin with, to contrast it with Leibnizian essentialism and mereological essentialism. I also want to bring out the connection of our theory of essentialism with an Aristotelean theory of natural kinds.

Aristotelean Essentialism and Leibnizian Essentialism

Leibniz, as is well known, had a very special doctrine about essentialism. One way of seeing its special nature is to consider an exchange of views between him and Arnauld in May of 1686. Arnauld argued to Leibniz that only some of the properties of an individual substance are essential (in his language, "part of the individual concept"). His argument was as follows:

> I have, therefore, only to consult it in order to know what is involved in this individual concept, just as I have only to consult the specific concept of a sphere to know what is involved there. . . . I am certain, that, inasmuch as I think, I am myself. But I am able to think that I will make a certain journey or that I will not, being perfectly assured that neither the one nor the other will prevent me from being myself. I maintain very decidedly that neither the one nor the other is involved in me.[19]

Leibniz, in response, argued that all the properties must be part of the concept:

> There is a great difference in the two cases for the concept of myself and of any other individual substance is infinitely more extended and more difficult to understand than is a specific concept like that of a sphere which is only incomplete. It is not sufficient that I feel myself as a substance which thinks; I must also distinctly conceive what distinguishes me from all other spirits.[20]

Arnauld, in his controversy with Leibniz, was using our definition of an essential property when he argued that even if I make a certain journey, the property of making that journey is not essential because there is, at an earlier stage, a possible future in which I continue to exist without having the property of making that journey. Leibniz's motives for rejecting Arnauld's arguments are less clear. The thought suggested at the end of the above quotation is this: my essential properties (the properties that are part of the concept of me) must include individuating characteristics, properties that distinguish me from all other actual and possible objects. It is these properties that someone thinks of when they think of me, and unless these properties distinguished me from all other possible objects, they wouldn't be thinking of me. Therefore, the property of making that journey must be essential to me (part of the concept of me), for if it were not, how would I be distinguished from that other possible object just like me except for not having made the journey?

The above interpretation of Leibniz is controversial, although I think correct, so I want to introduce as a technical term "Leibnizian essentialism," which will refer to the doctrine (whether or not held by Leibniz) that among the essential properties of an object are properties that individuate it from all other actual (and perhaps even possible) objects. What I would like to do is to show how our theory avoids, for the most part, Leibnizian essentialism. For the most part, properties that are essential on our account are kind-properties and not individuating properties.

Take the property of being in a given place p_1 at a given time t_1. At first glance, this seems to distinguish the object o_1 that had it from all other actual objects (but not from all other possible objects). It seems to be an individuating property. It is, however, clearly not essential to o_1. At some time, t_o, before t_1, there was a possible future in which o_1 was at t_1 at some place other than p_1. Again, take the property of being the first person to land on the moon. If there is some object o_1 that has that property, it is certainly the only actual object (but again not the only possible one) that has that property. It is therefore an individuating property. It is, however, clearly not essential to o_1. At some time t_o before t_1

there was a possible future in which o_1 was not the first person to land on the moon and yet continued to exist (a future, for example, in which he was ill and couldn't travel).

In general, then, individuating properties are not essential properties. There are, however, some difficulties here. Consider object o_1 and the property of-being-identical-with-o_1. Clearly, only o_1 among all actual and possible objects has this property. Moreover, it would seem that, by our account, o_1 has it essentially. After all, o_1 has the property of-being-identical-with-o_1, has always had that property, there is no possible past in which o_1 existed without being identical with o_1, and there is no moment of time at which o_1 is identical with o_1 and at which there is a possible future in which o_1 exists without being identical with o_1. So there is at least one property that satisfies the requirements of Leibnizian essentialism, and without some ad hoc restrictions on what counts as a property or as an essential property, I cannot see any basis for rejecting this conclusion.

Alvin Plantinga has argued that there are other types of properties, world-indexed properties, that are essential and individuating.[21] Consider, for example, some property P_1 that only o_1 has in w_1, and then consider the property of-having-P_1-in-w_1. The property in question is an individuating property, since it does distinguish o_1 from all other actual or possible objects (as opposed to the property of having P_1, which only distinguished it from actual objects). It would appear, moreover, to be an essential property. Now, as formulated, Plantinga is envisaging nonoverlapping possible worlds. But we can reformulate his example to deal with the property of-having-P_1-in-future-f_1 (a future of some actual moment). So we seem to have still another kind of property that satisfies the requirements of Leibnizian essentialism.

I am not much moved by Plantinga's argument, for I have serious doubts about the existence of these world-indexed properties or these future-indexed properties. They seem to be superfluous in our ontology. After all, for any object and any world-indexed property, there is a corresponding fact of that object's having the corresponding nonworld-indexed property in that world. If, for example, object a has the property of being-red-in-world-w_1, then there is the corresponding fact that a has in world w_1 the property of-being-red. Why, then, do we have to clutter up our ontology with these world-indexed properties? And if, of course, we have no reason to admit them into our ontology, we have no reason to accept them as individuating essential properties.

This point can also be put as follows: suppose we have in our ontology objects, properties, worlds, and facts. In particular, suppose we have in our ontology object a, the property of being red, world w_1, and the fact that a is red in w_1. I cannot see that adding to our ontology the property of-being-red-in-w_1 and the fact that a has that property accomplishes anything. The truth of "a is red in w_1" is due simply to a's having in w_1 the property of being red. And if we have no reason for adding them, it seems to follow that we have no reason for believing that they exist. So it is not clear then that there are these other properties that satisfy the requirements of Leibnizian essentialism.

Professor Plantinga has the following to say by way of explanation and defense of his world-indexed properties.

> Socrates has the property of being snubnosed in w, where w is a possible world, if and only if w includes Socrates's being snubnosed. If w is a world in which Socrates has the property of being snubnosed, then clearly enough Socrates has the property being snubnosed in w. It is not easy to see that this property merits much by way of scorn and contempt.[22]

As an explanation of what he has in mind by a world-indexed property, this is fine. Plantinga has said nothing, however, to justify his supposition that these properties exist.

It might seem that we are being arbitrary here. We have just admitted the existence of properties such as the property of-being-identical-with-o, and such properties are indeed crucial for our argument in Chapter One. Having done so, we then challenge the existence of Plantinga's world-indexed properties. What justifies this difference?

In both cases, the existence of the property in question is decided by reference to whether its existence is required in the account of the truth of certain claims. The presupposed theory of truth is that claims are true just in case the appropriate facts exist, and that these facts consist of objects having properties in given worlds at given times. We admit the property of-being-identical-with-o, because, for reasons summarized in Section 1.2, its existence seems required by the best account of the truth of the claim that $o_1 = o_1$. We reject the property of-being-snubnosed-in-w_1, just because, as we have just seen, it does not seem to be required for the truth of such claims as the claim that Socrates is snubnosed in w_1.

I conclude, therefore, that for the most part we have avoided Leibnizian essentialism and are committed for the most part only to an essentialism of kinds-properties.

Aristotelean Essentialism and Mereological Essentialism

There are those who maintain the thesis that the parts of an object are essential to that object. Put formally, their thesis, the thesis of mereological essentialism, is the thesis that:

For every x and y, if x is ever part of y,
then y is necessarily such that x is part
of y at any time that y exists.

In this section, we will consider the relation between this thesis of mereological essentialism and our Aristotelean approach to essentialism.

Consider the table on which I am writing and its top. Its top is, at this moment, a part of the table. It follows, according to the thesis of mereological essentialism, that this table has the property of having-this-top-as-one-of-its parts essentially, and has it essentially at all times at which it exists. At first glance, this seems just false. After all, there seem to be many possible futures in which I could have a different top on my table without my table's going out of existence. So how can the table have the property of having-this-top-as-one-of-its-parts essentially? Again, couldn't the people who make this table have made it with a different top? If they could have, then it would seem that there are possible pasts in which this table existed without this property. So it would seem that the table does not have the property of having-this-top-as-one-of-its-parts essentially.

Chisholm, who is the leading advocate of mereological essentialism, is well aware of this point.[23] He, however, only intends his thesis to apply to objects and their parts in the strict and philosophical sense. What he has in mind is this: people suppose that the ordinary objects of our discourse, such as tables, persist for substantial periods of time and change their parts. They conclude, therefore, that having the parts that they do have is not essential to them. In fact, however, this persistance is only persistance in a non-philosophical sense, and the objects and parts are only objects and parts in a nonphilosophical sense. Objects such as tables normally persist, in the strict philosophical sense, only for very short periods of time and go out of existence whenever a part is changed. Therefore, providing we speak strictly and philosophically, the thesis of mereological essentialism is correct for objects and their parts.

What then follows about mereological essentialism if we accept the Aristotelean approach? It depends upon what we say about the dispute between Chisholm and his opponents. If ordinary objects do persist, in a strict sense, for considerable periods of time even though their parts change, then the Aristotelean approach will entail the falsehood of mereological essentialism. If, however, Chisholm is right, then the Aristotelean approach will lead to the truth of mereological essentialism. In other words, Aristotelean essentialism is neutral on the question of mereological essentialism until such time as certain other issues are resolved.

Aristotelean Essentialism and the Theory of Natural Kinds

We have, in section 5.5 and so far in 5.6, developed our theory of essentialism by showing the sort of properties that are not essential according to our Aristotelean theory. We must now discuss which properties are essential according to our theory; in light of that discussion, we will also show the connection between our theory and the idea of a natural kind.

There are, of course, certain properties that everything has essentially. These include such properties as self-identity, as being-colored-if-red, and so on. There are also, as we saw earlier in this section, some essential properties had uniquely by a given object. For object *a*, for example, there is the property of being-identical-with-*a*, which only it has. But what other properties are had essentially?

Consider the piece of paper on which I am now writing. It is a yellow piece of paper. It does not have the property of being yellow essentially. It was, at first, a white piece of paper; so it has not always been yellow, and therefore it has the property of being yellow accidentally. It does, however, have the property of being a piece of paper essentially. It has been a piece of paper since it came into existence. In any possible future (of the present or of the past) in which it stopped being a piece of paper—say if it were burned into ashes—it would no longer exist. And there is no possible past in which it existed without being a piece of paper (if there were, its becoming a piece of paper would not have been its coming into existence, but it clearly is). So it seems to be a piece of paper essentially.

Consider the tree from which this paper was made. It had, at a certain time, *x* leaves. The property of having that number of leaves was clearly not essential. There were many possible futures in which it had a different number of leaves. It does, however, have the property of being a tree essentially. It has been a tree since it came into existence, in any possible future (of the present or of the past) in which it stopped being a tree—say if it were chopped down—it would no longer exist, and there is no possible past in which it existed without being a tree (if there were, its becoming a tree would not have been its coming into existence, which it clearly is).

These two examples, and many more that can be given, suggest that our theory of essentialism is a very Aristotelean theory, for these essential properties of an object correspond to the sort of thing an object is, correspond to the object's Aristotelean secondary substance. This is an extremely important point. In most recent discussions of essentialism, the emphasis has been on the connection between essential properties and the properties that an object must have necessarily. But there is traditionally this other important connection, the connection between the properties that an object has essentially and the sort of thing that it is. Our theory seems to capture this connection.

The picture that seems to be emerging of the essential properties of an object is this: there are certain essential properties had uniquely by a given object; there are certain sortal properties that it has essentially and that it shares with other objects; there are certain universal properties that it has essentially. This picture looks, of course, like a very classical picture of essentialism.

To see how classical and Aristotelean this picture is, we need to consider one further question. We shall say that any property had essentially by some object and accidentally by none determines a natural kind, and that the set of objects having that property is a natural kind. The question that we have to consider is whether all essential properties (properties had essentially by something) determine a natural kind. Equivalently, are there some properties that are had essentially by some objects and accidentally by others? If the answer to this first question is yes, then the connection between essentialism and the sort of a thing that an object is would be greatly strengthened.

A number of authors have argued that this connection cannot be maintained because the answer to our question is no. Alvin Plantinga, for example, has offered the following argument:[24] let P be some property had essentially by a but not at all by b, and let Q be some property had accidentally by b but not at all by a. Then the property of being either P or Q is had essentially by a and accidentally by b. So the claim that all essential properties determine natural kinds must be false. John Hooker has offered a different argument:[25] suppose, as seems reasonable, that ice cubes have the property of being an ice cube essentially. Then, they must also have the property of being a solid essentially. So the property of being a solid is an essential property. But does it really determine a natural kind? Aren't there some objects that merely possess that property accidentally, objects that could at a later stage become liquid or gaseous even if they are now solid? As impressive as these arguments may seem initially, I believe that both of them can be met and in the same way. Consider, first, Hooker's argument. Surely, the property of being a solid is part of the property of being an ice cube since, of necessity, nothing can be the latter without being the former. Similarly, in Plantinga's example, the property of being-either-P-or-Q is part of the property of being a P since, of necessity, nothing can be the latter without being the former. To maintain the classical connection between the theory of essentialism and the theory of natural kinds, we need only advance the connection in the following way: all essential properties either determine a natural kind or are part of an essential property that does determine a natural kind.

There is an alternative way of preserving the connection, one that ultimately goes back to a suggestion made by Jonathan Bennett. According to this suggestion, we need to modify the conditions under which an object a has P essentially so that all objects that have P, and not merely a, have it throughout their existence, there are no possible pasts in which they don't, and, for any moment at which they have it, there is no possible future in which they don't. Then, we can be sure that all essential properties determine a natural kind. I prefer our approach because, as Russell once said, it has the satisfaction of honest labor. Bennett's approach gets the desired results only by ruling out putative counterexamples as nonessential properties. Our approach avoids the counterexample without this definitional salvation.

Our thesis about the relation between essential properties has to be modified, however, so as to avoid triviality. After all, consider an essential property P that does not seem to determine a natural kind. It is part of the property having-P-essentially which certainly does determine a natural kind. So it would be trivially true, in a way that we don't want, that all essential properties either determine a natural kind or are part of an essential property that does determine a natural kind. The modification that I would propose is based upon distinguishing ordinary properties from modal properties (which are properties of having other properties necessarily or contingently). The nontrivial thesis that I would suggest as a modification is just this: all essential properties either determine a natural kind or are part of an essential nonmodal property that does determine a natural kind.

In short, then, our approach to essentialism is Aristotelean in two ways. It bases the essential-accidental distinction on the Aristotelean distinction between substantial change and mere alteration. More importantly, however, it produces a theory of essentialism that connects closely with an Aristotelean theory of natural kinds.

5.7 Concluding Remarks

We have in this chapter developed a theory of essentialism with a number of important characteristics: (a) it can be challenged only by those who would challenge the distinction between alterations and substantial changes; (b) it can meet the challenge of providing meaning for essentialist claims in light of a theory of identity across possible worlds; (c) it seems to result in objects having as essential the properties that seem intuitively essential and that seem to be connected to the sort of an object that it is.

Despite all of these desirable features, there remain important challenges to our theory. To begin with, and as has already been pointed out at the end of Chapter Four, can't we borrow our own arguments from Chapter Three (where we argued against a variety of additional necessary conditions) to show that the additional necessary conditions for identity through time that come along with a theory of essentialism are not really necessary? Second, how do we know that the claims that we have made about possible pasts and possible futures of particular objects are true? And if we don't know that they are true, how can we know which properties are had essentially? We shall see in the next and final chapter that these two questions can be answered by appealing to the same basic insight.

SIX ◆ ESSENCE AND EXPLANATION

Our final account in Chapter Five was that 'a has property P essentially' means 'a has P, a has always had P, there is no possible past in which a exists without P, and there is no moment of time at which a has had P and at which there is a possible future in which a exists without P.' Of these four conditions that must hold if a is to have P essentially, the first two seem to pose no special epistemological problems. The third and fourth conditions are different, and those who have epistemological doubts about essentialism will naturally focus their attention on these two conditions. How do we know, for example, that there is no possible past in which this tree exists without being a tree? We might say that this must be so because its becoming a tree must also be its coming into existence. But how do we know this? How, moreover, do we know that there is (and has been) no future at which this tree exists without being a tree? We might say that this must be so because its stopping to be a tree must also be its going out of existence. But how do we know this? More generally, how do we know which changes constitute comings-into-existence or goings-out-of-existence? This is the main question with which we will be struggling in this chapter. As was claimed at the end of Chapter Five, the answer to this question will serve as the basis for resolving some of the other problems left for the theory of essentialism.

6.1 Experience and Intuition

There are certain essential properties that pose no such epistemological problems. These are properties such as being self-identical or colored if red which everything must have at all times, and which every object therefore has essentially, given our definition. The epistemological problem with which we are concerned rises only for selectively essential properties, for properties that only some objects have essentially.

It is true that we cannot experience that, for example, there is no possible past in which this tree exists without being a tree, and that we also cannot experience that there is no possible future in which this tree exists without being a tree. But haven't we experienced trees coming into existence when they become trees, and going out of existence when they stop being trees? Couldn't these types of experiences be the epistemological foundations of essentialist claims?

This suggestion comes to the following: we observe an object coming into existence only as it acquires certain properties and going out of existence only as it loses them. We then see the same thing happening with other objects and those properties. On the basis of these observations, we infer that the acquisition of these properties constitute the coming-into-existence of any object that has them (so no such object has a possible past in which it exists without these properties), and that the loss of these properties constitute the going-out-of-existence of any object that has them (no such object has, at any time, a possible future in which it exists without these properties).

On this account, our knowledge of the essential properties of an object is empirical knowledge. This will, no doubt, make some suspect this account. After all, an object's having a property essentially is equivalent to its having it necessarily, and as Kant has pointed out, necessity is a mark of the a priori.

I cannot share these grounds of suspicion. The necessary truth of a proposition may well be a sign of the a prioricity of that proposition. Here, however, we are dealing with an object's having a property necessarily, with a de re necessity. Why must such necessities only be discoverable a priori? It should be noted that Aristotle, the founder of such theories, thought that our knowledge of basic essential properties was empirical (although the details of his account in the *Posterior Analytics* is very obscure).[1]

My difficulty is a different one. On this account, we are supposed to be able to see, for example, that a given tree has gone out of existence when it burns down and becomes a pile of ashes. Suppose, however, that someone claims that the tree still exists, that it is identical with the pile of ashes, although it is no longer a tree. Is it plausible to claim that we can just see that he is wrong? And if not, how can we say that we observe in any case that the tree goes out of existence when it stops being a tree? Doesn't this indicate that we have here something more than mere observation?

It is hard to make this argument into a conclusive refutation of our simple empiricist account. In order to do so, we would have to be able to draw a watertight distinction between what is observed and the interpretations we impose, and to show that the tree's going out of existence lies on the side of interpretation rather than observation. Nevertheless, the implausibilities appealed to above suggest that the straightforward empiricist account won't do.

One might go, of course, to the other extreme and suppose that our knowledge of the essential properties of objects is totally independent of our experience. One might claim, for example, that it is a rationally self-evident truth that a tree is necessarily a tree and goes out of existence when it stops being a tree. Now it is a rationally self-evident truth that "a tree is a tree" is a necessary truth. That is, however, irrelevant. The question before us is a different one, viz. whether it is rationally self-evident that a tree goes out of existence (as opposed to merely stopping to be a tree) when it stops being a tree. It is hard to see how the answer to this question can be yes, since it seems perfectly possible for a rational person to challenge the truth of this claim.

There seems, therefore, to be a fundamental epistemological difficulty about the conditions that make up the heart of any essentialist claim. I believe, however, that this challenge can be met once we go beyond observation reports and rationally self-evident truths. We need to take into account other sources of knowledge. In order to do so, however, we need to consider a question that we have so far avoided, viz. what is the role of essentialist claims in our broader cognitive activities? It is to this question that we turn in the next section. In dealing with it, however, we will have to deal with the broader problem of the nature of scientific explanations.

6.2 ARISTOTELEAN EXPLANATIONS

For some time, philosophers of science have recognized that Hempel's covering law model for scientific explanations leaves out something vital.[2] There are pairs of purported explanations of the same phenomenon, both members of which meet Hempel's requirements, but only one of which really is an explanation (or, at least, only one of which has significant explanatory strength). In a paper I published some years ago, I argued that one could solve this problem by introducing into the theory of explanation two notions, a nonconstant-conjunction notion of causality and an Aristotelean notion of essence.[3] I want to reargue that point here, for it is crucial for our solution to the epistemological questions about essentialism that the explanatory import of essential claims be noted.

Let us begin by considering the following explanation of why it is that sodium normally combines with chlorine in a ratio of one-to-one:

(A) (1) sodium normally combines with bromine in a ratio of one-to-one

(2) everything that normally combines with bromine in a ratio of one-to-one normally combines with chlorine in a ratio of one-to-one

(3) therefore, sodium normally combines with chlorine in a ratio of one-to-one.

This purported explanation meets all of the requirements laid down by Hempel's covering law model for scientific explanation. After all, the law to be explained is deduced from two other general laws that are true and have empirical content. Nevertheless, this purported explanation seems to have absolutely no explanatory power. And even if one were to say, as I think it would be wrong to say, that it does have at least a little explanatory power, why is it that it is not as good an explanation of the law in question (that sodium normally combines with chlorine in a ratio of one-to-one) as the explanation of that law in terms of the atomic structure of sodium and chlorine and the theory of chemical bonding? The covering law model, as it stands, seems to offer us no answer to that question.

A defender of the covering law model would, presumably, offer the following reply: both of these explanations, each of which meets the requirements of the model, are explanations of the law in question, but the explanation in terms of atomic structure is to be preferred to the explanation in terms of the way that sodium combines with bromine because the former contains in its explanans more powerful laws than the latter. The laws about atomic structure and the theory of bonding are more powerful than the law about the ratio with which sodium combines with bromine because more phenomena can be explained by the former than by the latter.

I find this answer highly unsatisfactory, partially because I don't see that (A) has any explanatory power at all. But that is not the real problem. The real problem is that this answer leaves something very mysterious. I can see why, on the grounds just mentioned, one would prefer to have laws like the ones about atomic structure rather than laws like the one about the ratio with which sodium and bromine combine. But why does that make explanations in terms of the latter type of laws less preferable? Or to put the question another way, why should laws that explain more explain better?

So much for my first problem for the covering-law model, a problem with its account of the way in which we explain scientific laws. An analogous problem can be raised, of course, for its account of how we explain particular events. I should now like to raise another problem for it, using an example dealing with the explanation of particular events. An analogous problem can be raised, of course, involving an example of an "explanation" of a scientific law. Consider the following three explanations:

(B) (1) if the temperature of a gas is constant, then its pressure is inversely proportional to its volume

(2) at time t_1, the volume of the container c was v_1 and the pressure of the gas in it was p_1

(3) the temperature of the gas in c did not change from t_1 to t_2

(4) the pressure of the gas in container c at t_2 is $2p_1$

(5) the volume of x at t_2 is $\frac{1}{2}v_1$.

(C) (1) if the temperature of a gas is constant, then its pressure is inversely proportional to its volume

(2) at time t_1, the volume of the container c was v_1 and the pressure of the gas in it was p_1

(3) the temperature of the gas in c did not change from t_1 to t_2

(4) the volume of the gas in container c at t_2 is $\frac{1}{2}v_1$

(5) the pressure of c at t_2 is $2p_1$.

(D) (1) if the temperature of a gas is constant, then its pressure is inversely proportional to its volume

(2) at time t_1, the volume of the container c was v_1 and the pressure of the gas in it was p_1

(3) the temperature of the gas in c did not change from t_1 to t_2

    (4)   by t_2, I had so compressed the container by pushing on it from all sides that its volume was $\frac{1}{2}v_1$

    (5)   the pressure of c at t_2 is $2p_1$

All three of these purported explanations meet all of the requirements of Hempel's model. The explanadum, in each case, is deducible from the explanans which, in each case, contains at least one true general law with empirical content. And yet, there are important differences between the three. My intuitions are that (B) is no explanation at all (thereby providing us with a clear counterexample to Hempel's model), that (C) is a poor explanation, and that (D) is a much better one. But if your intuitions are that (B) is still an explanation, even if not a very good one, that makes no difference for now. The important point is that there is a clear difference between the explanatory power of these three explanations, and the covering law model provides us with no clue as to what it is.

These problems and counterexamples are not isolated cases, and they led me to suspect that there is something fundamentally wrong with the whole covering law model and that a new approach to the understanding of scientific explanation is required. At the same time, however, I felt that this model, which fits so many cases and seems so reasonable, just couldn't be junked entirely. This left me in a serious dilemma, one that I only began to see my way out of after I realized that Aristotle, in the *Posterior Analytics,* had already seen these problems and had offered a solution to them, one that contained both elements of Hempel's model and some other elements entirely foreign to it. So let me begin my presentation of my solution to these problems by looking at some aspects of Aristotle's theory of scientific explanation.

Aristotle wanted to draw a distinction between knowledge of the fact (knowledge that p is so) and knowledge of the reasoned fact (knowledge why p is so) and he did so by asking us to consider the following two arguments, the former of which only provides us with knowledge of the fact, while the latter of which provides us with knowledge of the reasoned fact:

(E) (1) the planets do not twinkle
    (2) all objects that do not twinkle are near the earth
    (3) therefore, the planets are near the earth.

(F) (1) the planets are near the earth
    (2) all objects that are near the earth do not twinkle
    (3) therefore, the planets do not twinkle.

The interesting thing about this point, for our purposes, is that while both of these arguments fit Hempel's model, only one of them, as Aristotle already saw, provides us with an explanation of its conclusion. Moreover, his account of why this is so seems just right:

> of two reciprocally predicable terms the one which is not the cause may quite easily be the better known and so become the middle term of the demonstration. . . . This syllogism, then, proves not the reasoned fact but only the fact; since they are not near because they do not twinkle. The major and middle of the proof, however, may be reversed, and then the demonstration will be of the reasoned fact . . . since its middle term is the proximate cause.[4]

In other words, nearness is the cause of not twinkling, and not vice versa, so the nearness of the planets to the earth explains why they do not twinkle, but their not twinkling does not explain why they are near the earth.

It is important to note that such an account is incompatible with the logical empiricists' theory of causality as constant conjunction. After all, given the truth of the premises of (E) and (F), nearness and nontwinkling are each necessary and sufficient for each other, so, on the constant conjunction account, each is equally the cause of the other. And even if the constant conjunction account is supplemented in any of the usual ways, nearness and nontwinkling would still equally be the cause of each other. After all, both "all near celestial objects twinkle" and "all twinkling celestial objects are near" contain purely qualitative predicates, have a potentially infinite scope, are deducible from higher-order scientific generalizations, and support counterfactuals. In other words, both of these generalizations are lawlike generalizations, and not mere accidental ones, so each of the events in question is, on a sophisticated Humean account, the cause of the other. So Aristotle's account presupposes the falsity of the constant conjunction account of causality. But that is okay. After all, the very example that we are dealing with now, where nearness is clearly the cause of nontwinkling but not vice versa, shows us that the constant conjunction theory of causality (even in its normal more sophisticated versions) is false.

Now if we apply Aristotle's account to our example with the gas, we get a satisfactory account of what is involved there. The decrease in volume (due, itself, to my pressing on the container from all sides) is the cause of the increase in pressure, but not vice versa, so the former explains the latter, but not vice versa. And Aristotle's account also explains a phenomenon called to our attention by Bromberger,[5] viz. that while we can deduce both the height of a flagpole from the length of the shadow it casts and the position of the sun in the sky, and the length of the shadow it casts from the height of the flagpole and the position of the sun in the sky, only the latter deduction can be used in an explanation. It is easy to see why this is so; it is the sun striking at a given angle the flagpole of the given height that causes its shadow to have the length that it does, but the sun striking the flagpole when its shadow has the length of the shadow is surely not the cause of the height of the flagpole.

Generalizing this point, we can add a new requirement for explanation: a deductive-nomological explanation of a particular event is a satisfactory explanation of the event when (besides meeting all of Hempel's requirements) its explanans contain essentially a description of the event which is the cause of the event described in the explanandum. If they do not, then it may not be a satisfactory explanation. And similarly, a deductive-nomological explanation of a law is a satisfactory explanation of that law when (besides meeting all of Hempel's requirements) every event which is a case of the law to be explained is caused by an event which is a case of one (in each case, the same) of the laws contained essentially in the explanans.

It might be thought that what we have said so far is sufficient to explain why it is that (A) is not an explanation, and why it is that the explanation of sodium and chlorine's combining in a one-to-one ratio in terms of the atomic structure of sodium and chlorine is an explanation. After all, no event which is a case of sodium and chlorine combining in a one-to-one ratio is caused by any event which is a case of sodium and bromine combining in a one-to-one ratio. So, given our requirements, deduction (A), even though it meets all of Hempel's requirements, need not be (and indeed is not) an explanation. But every event which is a case of sodium and chlorine combining in a one-to-one ratio is caused by the sodium and chlorine in question having the atomic structure that they do (after all, if they had a different atomic structure, they would combine in a different ratio). So an explanation involving the atomic structure would meet our new requirement and would therefore be satisfactory.

The trouble with this account is that it incorrectly presupposes that it is the atomic structure of sodium and chlorine that causes them to combine in a one-to-one ratio. A whole essay would be required to show, in detail, what is wrong with this presupposition; I can, here, only briefly indicate the trouble and hope that this brief indication will be sufficient for now: a given case of sodium combining with chlorine is the same event as that sodium combining with that chlorine in a one-to-one ratio, and, like all other events, that event has only one cause. It is, perhaps, that event which brings it about that the sodium and chlorine are in proximity to each other under the right conditions. That is the cause of the event in question, and not the atomic structure of the sodium and chlorine in question (which, after all, were present long before they combined). To be sure, these atomic structures help explain one aspect of the event in question, the ratio in which they combine, but that does not make them the cause of the event.

To say that the atomic structure of the atoms in question is not the cause of their combining in a one-to-one ratio is *not* to say that a description of that structure is not an essential part of any causal explanation of their combining. It obviously is. But equally well, to say that a description of it is a necessary part of any causal explanation is *not* to say that it is (or is part of) the cause of their combining. There is a difference, after all, between causal explanations and causes, and between parts of the former and parts of the latter. Similarly, to say that the atomic structure is not the cause of their combining is *not* to say that that event had no cause; indeed, we suggested one (the event that brought about the proximity of the atoms), and others can also be suggested (the event of the atoms acquiring certain specific electrical and quantum mechanical properties). It is only to say that the atomic structure is not the cause.

Keeping these two points in mind, we can see that all that we said before was that the perfectly satisfactory explanation, in terms of the atomic structure of the atoms, of their combining in a one-to-one ratio does not meet the condition just proposed because it contains no description of the event that caused the combining to take place. But since it obviously is a good explanation, some additional types of explanations must be allowed for.

So, Aristotle's first suggestion, while quite helpful in solving some of our problems, does not solve all of them. There is, however, another important suggestion that he makes that will, I believe, solve the rest of them. Aristotle says:

Demonstrative knowledge must rest on necessary basic truths; for the object of scientific knowledge cannot be other than it is. Now attributes attaching essentially to their subjects attach necessarily to them. . . . It follows from this that premises of the demonstrative syllogism must be connections essential in the sense explained: for all attributes must inhere essentially or else be accidental, and accidental attributes are not necessary to their subjects.[6]

There are many aspects of this passage that I do not want to discuss now. But one part of it seems to me to suggest a solution to our problem. It is the suggestion that a demonstration can be used as an explanation (can provide us with "scientific knowledge") when at least one of the explanans essential to the derivation states that a certain class of objects has a certain property, and (although the explanans need not state this) that property is possessed by those objects essentially.

Let us, following that suggestion, now look at our two proposed explanations as to why sodium combines with chlorine in a ratio of one to one. In one of them, we are supposed to explain this in terms of the fact that sodium combines with bromine in a one-to-one ratio. In the other explanation, we are supposed to explain this in terms of the atomic structure of sodium and chlorine. Now in both of these cases, we can demonstrate from the fact in question (and certain additional facts) that sodium does combine with chlorine in a one-to-one ratio. But there is an important difference between these two proposed explanations. The atomic structure of some chunk of sodium or mass of chlorine is an essential property of that object. If the structure of an atom changes, it would be (numerically) a different object. But the fact that it combines with bromine in a one-to-one ratio is not an essential property of the sodium chunk, although it may be true of every chunk of sodium. One can, after all, imagine situations in which it would not combine in that ratio but in which it would still be (numerically) the same object. Therefore, one of our explanans, the one describing the atomic structure of sodium and chlorine, contains a statement that attributes to the sodium and chlorine a property which is an essential property of that sodium and chlorine (even if the statement does not say that it is an essential property), while the other of our explanans, the one describing the way in which sodium combines with bromine, does not. And it is for just this reason that the former explanans, but not the latter, explains the phenomenon in question.

Generalizing this Aristotelean point, we can set down another requirement for explanations as follows: a deductive-nomological explanation of a particular event is a satisfactory explanation of that event when (besides meeting all of Hempel's requirements) its explanans contains essentially a statement attributing to a certain class of objects a property had essentially by that class of objects (even if the statement does not say that they have it essentially), and when at least one object involved in the event described in the explanandum is a member of that class of objects. If this requirement is unfulfilled, then it may not be a satisfactory explanation. And similarly, a deductive-nomological explanation of a law is a satisfactory explanation of that law when (besides meeting all of Hempel's requirements) each event that is a case of the law which is the explanadum, involves an entity that is a member of a class (in each case, the same class) such that the explanans contain a statement attributing to that class a property that each of its members has essentially (even if the statement does not say that they have it essentially).

It is important to note that such an account is incompatible with the logical empiricist conception of theoretical statements as instruments and not as statements describing the world. For after all, many of these essential attributions are going to be theoretical statements, and they can hardly be statements attributing to a class of objects an essential property if they aren't really statements at all. But that is all right, for it just gives us one more reason for rejecting an account more notable for the audacity of its proponents in proposing it than for its plausibility or for the illumination it casts.

Naturally, a full defense of this Aristotelean theory of explanation requires a discussion of both non-constant-conjunction causality and of essentialism. For our purposes, however, we will merely focus on the role of essential properties in explanation.

What happens when we explain the occurrence of some event by attributing to some object involved in that event the possession of a certain property that it has essentially? The crucial point is that we have invoked in our explanans something that requires no further explanation. The given object's possession of the given property requires no further explanation, since the object comes into existence only when it possesses that property, and goes out of existence when it stops having that property. There is no difficulty, then, in understanding why it has that property; it cannot not have it.

It is precisely this feature of essential explanations that has led Popper to criticize them:

> The essentialist doctrine that I am contesting is solely the doctrine that science aims at ultimate explanation; that is to say, an explanation which (essentially, or, by its very nature) cannot be further explained, and which is in no need of any further explanation. Thus my criticism of essentialism does not aim at establishing the nonexistence of essences; it merely aims at showing the obscurantist character of the role played by the idea of essences in the Galilean philosophy of science.[7]

Popper's point really is very simple. If our explanans contain a statement describing essential properties (such as that sodium has the following atomic structure . . .), then there is nothing more to be said by way of explaining these explanans themselves. After all, what could we say by way of answering the question "why does sodium contain the atomic structure that it does?" So the use of essential explanations leads us to unexplainable explanans, and therefore to no new insights gained in the search for explanations of these explanans, and therefore to scientific sterility. Therefore, science should reject essential explanations.

There are, I believe, two things wrong with this objection. To begin with, Popper assumes that essential explanations will involve unexplainable explanans, and this is usually only partially true. Consider, after all, our explanation of sodium's combining with chlorine in a one-to-one ratio in terms of the atomic structure of sodium and chlorine. The explanans of that explanation, besides containing statements attributing to sodium and chlorine their essences (viz. their atomic number), also contain the general principles of chemical bonding, and these are not unexplainable explanans since they are not claims about essences. In general, even essential explanations leave us with some part (usually the most interesting part) of their explanans to explain, and they do not therefore lead to sterility in future enquiry. But, in addition, even if we did have an essential explanation all of whose explanans were essential statements and therefore unexplainable explanans, what are we to do, according to Popper? Should we reject the explanation? Should we keep it but believe that it is not an essential explanation? Neither of these strategies seems very plausible in those cases in which we have good reasons both for supposing that the explanation is correct and for supposing that the explanans do describe the essential properties of the objects in question. It cannot, after all, be a good scientific strategy to reject what we have good reasons to accept. So even if Popper's claim about their sterility for future scientific enquiry is true for some essential explanations, I cannot see that it gives us any reasons for rejecting these explanations, or for rejecting their claim to be essential explanations, when these explanations and claims are empirically well supported.

There is, of course, a certain point to Popper's objection, a point that I gladly concede. As is shown by his example from the history of gravitational theory, people may rush to treat a property as essential without adequate empirical evidence for that claim, and then it may turn out that they were wrong. They may even have good evidence for the claim that the property is essential and still be wrong. In either case, enquiry has been blocked where it should not have been blocked. We should certainly, therefore, be cautious in making claims about essential properties, and should, even when we make them on the basis of good evidence, realize that they may still be wrong. But these words of caution are equally applicable to all scientific claims; the havoc wreaked by false theories that lead enquiry along mistaken paths can be as bad as the havoc wreaked by false essential claims that block enquiry. And since they are only words of caution, they should not lead us to give up either theoretical explanations in general or essential explanations in particular.

Van Fraassen, in his recent survey of the problem of these explanatory assymetries, was favorably disposed toward our theory of explanation, but he rejected it at the end because:

> I do not see how he [Brody] would distinguish between the questions why the uranium atom disintegrated and why it disintegrated just then. In addition there is the problem that modern science is not formulated in terms of causes and essences, and it seems doubtful that these concepts can be redefined in terms which do occur there.[8]

I believe that both of these objections can be met. The second misunderstands our proposal. It is not required that the explanation describe some event as a cause or some property as essential. It is merely required that the explanation refer to an event that is, in fact, a cause, or to a property that is, in fact, essential. This is why modern science need not be formulated in terms of causes and essences. Moreover, if our account in Chapter Five is correct, then there is (at least) no problem of defining the concept of an essential property.

The first objection raises more serious questions, but it

can be met. Consider the event that is the disintegration of that uranium atom, and the event that is its disintegration just then. If our theory of event-identity is correct, then they are the same event, which either has the same cause or has no cause (and the latter is, of course, probably the case). In explaining why it disintegrated, then, we will have to refer not to its cause but to a statistical structure, using a Salmon-like statistical explanation.[9] Would such an explanation also be an explanation of why it disintegrated just then, or would it not? That depends on whether you adopt Salmon's proposal as it stands or add to it a pragmatic element of the type advocated by Van Fraassen. It seems to me, however, that that question is independent of the merits of our proposal.

To summarize, then: attributing a certain property to an object when the object has that property essentially means that we have a potential explanans that requires no further explanation. And when we can use such an explanans, we have an explanation that has a strong explanatory impact, precisely because it has an element with an explanatory finality about it. What I shall argue in the next section is that this explanatory role of essential attribution is crucial to the epistemology of essentialism.

6.3 HYPOTHESES ABOUT ESSENCES

Suppose that we find ourselves in the following position: the claim that an object a has a property P plays a role in a wide variety of Hempel-like explanations (that is, weak explanations or merely purported explanations) of the properties of a, but we have no explanation of why a has property P. In such a position, it seems to me that we may reasonably hypothesize that object a has property P essentially. Putting forward this hypothesis is justified in part because it leads to strong explanations of a's possessing those properties, and in part because it solves the problem of why a has property P.

How reasonable will it be to put forward this hypothesis

that a has P essentially? All other things being equal, its reasonableness will be proportional to the extent that we can, as a result, use a's possession of P to explain a's other properties; the more such phenomena that can be explained, the more reasonable the hypothesis. Again, all other things being equal, its reasonableness will be proportional to the seriousness of the previous failure to explain a's possession of P; the longer and harder the scientific community has tried and failed, the more reasonable will be the hypothesis that a has P essentially.

On this account, our claims about essential properties are empirical hypotheses open to confirmation and disconfirmation. However, the confirmation or disconfirmation is not a result of our observing the conditions under which objects come into existence or go out of existence. We have already indicated, in Section 6.1, why this empiricist account of our knowledge of essences is implausible. Instead, the confirmation or disconfirmation is an indirect one, based upon our assessment of certain explanatory accounts.

This last point can also be put as follows: when we first looked at an empiricist approach to our knowledge of essential properties, we supposed that we could learn about essential properties by generalizing from our experiences about when objects come into existence and go out of existence. The difficulty with this account was that it presupposed that we could report the experience of objects coming into existence and going out of existence, and it seems that such claims are interpretations (whose justification remained unclear) of what we experience, and not reports of what we experience. Our current empiricist approach differs by viewing hypotheses about the essential properties of objects as explanatory hypotheses. Having adopted such a hypothesis, we can then justifiably interpret our experience of the objects acquiring that property as an experience of their coming into existence, and we can justifiably interpret our experience of the objects losing that property as an experience of their going out of existence.

It is crucial to keep in mind that there are two factors that we consider when evaluating the hypothesis that a has P essentially, the explanatory value of a's having P, and the inability to explain otherwise why a has P. Consider, for example, a given object a that has a mass m_1. No doubt, a's having mass m_1 can be used in many Hempelian explanations of facts about a, but we certainly would not want to claim that a has m_1 essentially (a can, after all, change its mass without going out of existence). The justification for rejecting that claim is that we can provide an alternative causal explanation of a's acquiring m_1. The existence of this alternative explanation seriously weakens the claim that a has m_1 essentially.

One final point has to be made here. By our account, any claim that some object a has some property P essentially is supported by a variety of empirical claims, but has a content that differs from the content of those claims. This means that the empirical claims might be true, although the essentialist claim is false. And there is nothing in our account that rules out the possibility that we might come to have reasons to believe that this is the case, and that, despite the strong evidence for it, we should reject the essentialist hypothesis. This is crucial to keep in mind, as we shall see in the next section.

6.4 ESSENTIALISM AND FURTHER CONDITIONS FOR IDENTITY THROUGH TIME

In light of what we have said about the epistemology and logic of essentialist claims, we are now in a position to deal with a final problem that we first raised in Section 4.2. We pointed out then how the adoption of an essentialist claim introduced certain additional conditions on identity through time. Consider object o_1 existing at t_1 and object o_2 existing at t_2. Given the definition of "identity," o_1 and o_2 are identical just if, at any given time, they have all their properties at that time in common. Nothing is required about having some property both at t_1 and t_2. But now suppose that o_1 has P essentially. Then it can only continue to exist at t_2 and be identical with o_2 at t_2 just if it (and o_2) has P at t_2. So essentialist claims introduce additional necessary conditions for identity through time.

There are a number of difficulties that might be raised about these additional necessary conditions. To begin with, one might challenge them (as we challenged in Section 3.1 the claim that spatiotemporal continuity is an additional necessary condition for the identity of physical objects through time) on the grounds that there is no justification for imposing these requirements. This challenge can, however, be met easily. After all, any justification for the essentialist claim is also a justification for the additional necessary condition. Since we have already seen that there are conditions under which we would be justified in putting forward an essentialist claim, we have also seen that there are conditions under which we would have empirical justification for putting forward these additional necessary conditions. There is, however, a more substantial difficulty—also parallel to one we raised in Section 3.1—that requires further discussion.

Suppose we found ourselves in the following situation: we had powerful reasons for supposing that object o_1 at t_1 is identical with o_2 at t_2, powerful empirical reasons for supposing that they have all of their properties in common. Suppose, moreover, that we have powerful empirical reasons for believing that o_1 at t_1 has property P, and that objects which have P have it essentially. Suppose, finally, that we have powerful empirical reasons for supposing that o_2 at t_2 does not have property P. On our account, won't we then have powerful empirical reasons for believing both that $o_1 = o_2$ and that $o_1 \neq o_2$? This is the type of difficulty to which we open ourselves when we impose these additional necessary conditions. And, it might be claimed, we have therefore good reasons for not imposing these conditions.

Although more substantial than the first objection, this second objection can be met. To begin with, any evidence we have that o_1 has P essentially is evidence that this set of suppositions will not be jointly satisfied and that we will not encounter these difficulties. But suppose we did. All that we could conclude is that some of our evidence, however powerful, is misleading. Which evidence it is would require further empirical investigation. Even if that investigation showed that it was the evidence for the essentialist claim, that would provide no problem for us. As we saw at the end of Section 6.3, we might well have conditions under which we would be justified in concluding that, despite the powerful empirical evidence for them, our essentialist claims might be false. I conclude, therefore, that, given a proper understanding of the logic of evidence for essentialist claims, their implications for identity through time pose no problem.

◆ NOTES

One ◆ The Theory of Identity for Enduring Objects

1. See, for example, B. A. O. Williams, "Personal Identity and Individuation," *Proceedings of the Aristotelean Society*, 57 (1956–1957), 230.

2. Some of the most recent debate is collected in John Perry's *Personal Identity* (Berkeley and Los Angeles: University of California Press, 1975).

3. The most notable proponent of this position has been W. V. O. Quine. See, for example, his *Word and Object* (Cambridge: M.I.T. Press, 1960), p. 209.

4. Their claim is discussed in H. Putnam's, "It Ain't Necessarily So," *Journal of Philosophy*, 59 (1962), 658–671.

5. A prominent proponent of this claim is A. Flew in his articles, "Locke and the Problem of Personal Identity," *Philosophy*, 26 (1951), 53–68 and " 'The Soul' of Mr. A. M. Quinton," *The Journal of Philosophy*, 60 (1963), 337–344.

6. A. M. Quinton, "The Soul," *Journal of Philosophy*, 59 (1962), 393–409.

7. Quine, *Word and Object*.

8. D. Wiggins, *Identity and Spatio-Temporal Continuity* (Oxford: Basil Blackwell, 1967), is an extensive treatment of this additional claim.

9. See, for example, D. J. O'Connor, "The Identity of Indiscernibles," *Analysis* (1954) reprinted in M. Loux, *Universals and Particulars* (Garden City: Anchor Books, 1970), p. 227.

10. In "The Identity of Indiscernibles," reprinted in his *Philosophical Essays* (London: Macmillan, 1954).

11. O'Connor, "Identity."

12. Ayer, "Identity of Indiscernibles," p. 29.

13. Our defense of impredicativity in these paragraphs is indebted to R. Carnap's "The Logicist Foundations of Mathematics," reprinted in P. Benacerraf and H. Putnam, *Philosophy of Mathematics* (Englewood Cliffs: Prentice-Hall, 1964).

14. Wiggins, *Identity*, p. 34.

15. This example has been used extensively by D. Davidson in his essays about the identity of events.

16. J. Locke, *Essay Concerning Human Understanding,* edited by J. Yolton (London: Everyman, 1971), p. 275.

17. P. Geach, "Identity," in *Logic Matters* (Oxford: Blackwell, 1972), p. 240.

18. In M. Black, "Identity of Indiscernibles," reprinted in M. Loux, *Universals and Particulars* (Garden City: Anchor Books, 1970), p. 207.

19. *Ibid.,* p. 206.

20. *Ibid.,* p. 216.

21. Such a line of thought is suggested by John Perry in his introduction to his anthology, *Personal Identity,* pp. 6–11. I cannot see, however, that he has given us any reasons for not beginning in the case of persons, as opposed to baseball games, with names for enduring objects. We shall discuss his reasons further in Section 2.2.

Two • ENDURING AND NONENDURING OBJECTS

1. P. F. Strawson, *Individuals* (London: Methuen, 1957), chapter 1.

2. *Ibid.,* p. 16.

3. *Ibid.,* p. 21.

4. *Ibid.,* p. 57.

5. *Ibid.,* p. 51.

6. All of our references will be to the English translation by Rolf A. George, *The Logical Structure of the World* (London: Routledge and Kegan Paul, 1967).

7. N. Goodman, "Significance of Der Logische Aufbau," in P. A. Schlipp, *The Philosophy of Rudolf Carnap* (LaSalle, Ind.: Open Court, 1963), pp. 546–547.

8. Carnap, *Logical Structure,* pp. 88–89.

9. J. Perry, "Personal Identity, Memory, and the Problem of Circularity," in his *Personal Identity* (Berkeley and Los Angeles: University of California Press, 1975), p. 137.

THREE • IMPLICATIONS

1. N. R. Hanson, "The Dematerialization of Matter," in E. McMullin, *The Concept of Matter* (Notre Dame: University of Notre Dame Press, 1963), p. 556.

2. In his essay, "Identity and Spatio-temporal Continuity," in M. Munitz, *Identity and Individuation* (New York: New York University Press, 1971).

3. *Ibid.*, p. 53.

4. *Ibid.*, p. 101.

5. A. Flew, in his "Locke and the Problem of Personal Identity," *Philosophy*, 26 (1951), 53–68, correctly saw how these problem cases are the best tests for any theory of personal identity.

6. In his paper, "Personal Identity."

7. R. G. Swinburne, "Personal Identity," *Proceedings of the Aristotelian Society*, suppl. vol. (1973–1974), p. 240.

8. *Ibid.*, p. 241.

9. For example, Flew, "Locke."

10. *Ibid.*, p. 66.

11. In his 1957 essay, "Personal Identity and Individuation." All of our references will be to the reprinted essay in his book, *Problems of the Self* (Cambridge: Cambridge University Press, 1973).

12. *Ibid.*, p. 19.

13. *Ibid.*, pp. 23–24.

14. In A. Prior, "Opposite Number," *Review of Metaphysics*, 11 (1957–1958), 196–201.

15. In J. Perry, "Can the Self Divide," *Journal of Philosophy*, 69 (1972), 463–488.

16. In D. Parfit, "Personal Identity," *Philosophical Review*, 80 (1971), 3–27.

17. Quine, *Word and Object*, p. 209.

18. See, for example, A. Fraenkel and Y. Bar-Hillel, *Foundations of Set Theory* (Amsterdam: North Holland, 1958), pp. 27–33.

19. A. Goldman, *A Theory of Human Action* (Englewood Cliffs: Prentice-Hall, 1970).

20. This view is defended in "The Individuation of Events," in N. Rescher, *Essays in Honor of Carl G. Hempel* (Dordrecht: Reidel, 1969).

21. M. Beardsley, "Actions and Events," *American Philosophical Quarterly*, 12 (1975), 272.

22. In such essays as J. Kim, "Events and Their Descriptions: Some Considerations," in N. Rescher, *Essays.*

23. J. J. Thomson, "Individuating Actions," *Journal of Philosophy*, 68 (1971), 774–781. Beardsley, "Actions and Events."

Four ◆ The Theory of Change

1. Aristotle, *On Generation and Corruption*, 319ᵇ8–24.
2. Defended, for example, in E. Meyerson, *Identity and Reality* (London: George Allen and Unwin, 1930).
3. Aristotle, *Generation*, 320ᵃ2–4.
4. Suggested by Jack Meiland (in correspondence).
5. M. Price, "Identity through Time," *Journal of Philosophy*, 74 (1977), 201–217.
6. *Ibid.*, p. 203.
7. *Ibid.*, p. 210.
8. *Ibid.*, p. 212.
9. J. Locke, *Essay Concerning Human Understanding*, edited by J. Yolton (London: Everyman, 1971), pp. 274–275.
10. T. Reid, *Essays on the Intellectual Powers of Man* (Cambridge: M.I.T. Press, 1969), p. 340.

Five ◆ The Theory of Essentialism

1. The first two of these objections are due to W. V. O. Quine and are discussed by him in, among other places, *Word and Object* (Cambridge: M.I.T. Press, 1960), pp. 195–200. The third arises out of R. Chisholm, "Identity through Possible Worlds," *Nous*, 1 (1967), 1–8.
2. The crucial papers were R. Cartwright, "Some Remarks on Essentialism," *Journal of Philosophy*, 65 (1968), 615–627, and A. Plantinga, "De Re et De Dicto," *Nous*, 3 (1969), 235–258.
3. K. Fine, "Model Theory for Modal Logic," *Journal of Philosophical Logic*, 7 (1978), 125–156.
4. Alvin Plantinga, *The Nature of Necessity* (Oxford: Oxford University Press, 1974), p. 93.
5. *Ibid.*, p. 96.
6. D. Kaplan, "Quantifying In," in D. Davidson, and J. Hintikka, *Words and Objections* (Dordrecht: Reidel, 1969); and A. Plantinga, "De Re"; "World and Essence," *Philosophical Review*, 79 (1970), 461–492; and *Nature of Necessity*.
7. Plantinga, "De Re," p. 248.
8. See, for example, R. Adams, "Theories of Actuality," *Nous*, 8 (1974), 211–232; and F. Mondadori and A. Morton, "Modal Realism," *Philosophical Review*, 85 (1976), 3–20.
9. Chisholm, "Identity."
10. D. Lewis, "Counterpart Theory and Quantified Modal Logic," *Journal of Philosophy*, 65 (1968), 113–126.

11. F. Feldman, "Counterparts," *Journal of Philosophy* (1971); and A. Plantinga, *Nature of Necessity,* pp. 102–120.

12. In "Identity and Necessity," in M. Munitz, *Identity and Individuation* (New York: N.Y.U. Press, 1971), and in "Naming and Necessity," in D. Davidson and G. Harman, *Semantics of Natural Language* (Dordrecht: Reidel, 1972).

13. Kripke, "Naming and Necessity," p. 270.

14. *Ibid.,* p. 267.

15. R. Adams, "Primitive Thisness and Primitive Identity," *Journal of Philosophy,* 76 (1979), 5–26.

16. D. Kaplan, "Quantifying In," p. 224.

17. In conversation.

18. "Naming and Necessity," p. 351.

19. G. Leibniz, *Basic Writings* (LaSalle: Open Court, 1968), p. 98.

20. *Ibid.,* p. 126.

21. Plantinga, *Nature of Necessity,* pp. 44–87.

22. *Ibid.,* p. 64.

23. In his recent book, R. Chisholm, *Person and Object* (London: George Allen and Unwin, 1976), pp. 148–58.

24. Plantinga, "World and Essence," p. 465.

25. In conversation.

Six ◆ Essence and Explanation

1. In Book II, Chapter 19.

2. A good summary of this problem is found in B. van Frassen, "The Pragmatics of Explanation," *American Philosophical Quarterly,* 14 (1977), 143–151.

3. B. A. Brody, "Towards an Aristotelean Theory of Scientific Explanation," *Philosophy of Science,* 39 (1971), 20–31.

4. 78ᵃ28–78ᵇ3.

5. S. Bromberger, "Why Questions," in R. Colodny, *Mind and Cosmos* (Pittsburgh: University of Pittsburgh Press, 1966).

6. 74ᵇ5–12.

7. K. R. Popper, *Conjectures and Refutations* (London: Routledge and Kegan Paul, 1963), p. 105.

8. "Pragmatics," p. 147.

9. Salmon's views are found in W. Salmon, "Statistical Explanation," in R. G. Colodny, *Nature and Function of Scientific Theories* (Pittsburgh: University of Pittsburgh Press, 1970).

◆ INDEX

Library of Congress Cataloging in Publication Data

Brody, Baruch A
   Identity and essence.

   Includes index.
   1. Identity. 2. Essence (Philosophy) 3. Object
(Philosophy) I. Title.
BD236.B76   111   80-7511
ISBN 0-691-07256-6
ISBN 0-691-02013-2 (pbk.)